First published in 2019 by Tim Easton
Brisbane, Australia
Contact: tjeaston3@gmail.com

Copyright © 2019 Tim Easton

All rights reserved. Except as permitted under the Australian Copyright Act 1968, no part of this publication may be reproduced, stored in a retrieval system, or transmitted in any form or by any means, electronic, mechanical, photocopying, recording or otherwise, without prior written permission. All enquiries should be made to the author.

Author: Tim Easton
Twenty-One Days in the Himalayas
ISBN: 978 0 6484636 0 3

Subjects: Travel | Memoir
Book design: Jennifer Hall – **jellyfishcreative.com.au**
Publishing services: Bev Ryan – **bevryanpublishing.com**
Cover photo: *Annapurna I from the base camp* taken by Tim Easton
Previous page photo: *Pokhara pumpkin New Year's Eve carving* taken by Tim Easton

DISCLAIMER

Every effort has been made to ensure this book is free from error and omission and has been kept up to date. The information in this publication is of a general nature only and does not take into account personal needs, objectives or current situation. It should not be considered advice. The intent is to offer a variety of information to the reader. However, the author, publisher, editor or their agents or representatives shall not accept responsibility for any loss or inconvenience caused to a person or organisation relying on this information. Except as required by law, the author and publisher, their licensee, their entities, directors and employees do not accept any liability for any person acting, or refraining from acting, as a result of material in this book. The names of the people referred to in the case studies are not real and have been changed to maintain their privacy. We strongly recommend that professional advice is taken before making any decisions regarding personal needs.

CONTENTS

ACKNOWLEDGEMENTS   4
TIBETAN PRAYER FLAGS   5
FOREWORD   6
PROLOGUE   7

CHAPTER 01 — PAGE 8

CHAPTER 02 — PAGE 36

CHAPTER 03 — PAGE 54

CHAPTER 04 — PAGE 78

CHAPTER 05 — PAGE 102

POSTSCRIPT   147
MAP   148
REFERENCES   149
ADDENDUM   150
ABOUT THE AUTHOR   152

> "UNLIKE A METEOR HURTLING TO EARTH, WE HAVE THE OPTION OF TURNING OURSELVES AROUND. OUR IMPERATIVE IS TO RESCUE OURSELVES, FROM OURSELVES, BY OURSELVES. WE CAN NO MORE ESCAPE THIS RESPONSIBILITY THAN WE CAN ESCAPE OUR BIRTH ON EARTH."
>
> Bob Brown

ACKNOWLEDGEMENTS

I find this a very challenging section to write for fear of leaving someone out – and it would be very fair to say that many hundreds of people helped me to do this trek and create this book for public knowledge – but here we go!

My father most certainly, for his ability to 'get the job done'! No matter what the task there is nothing like British Army training to organise and carry out an expedition of any size and shape – even if it is one generation removed. My interest in language was most likely sparked by my father: he had a very good command of the English language, studied it part-time at the University of Queensland, and could once speak Latin, French and some Italian.

My mother, for her understanding and acceptance of the world – and particularly those of different cultures. It is my mother who has taught me to always try to walk with peace in this world. It was my father who taught me to stand my ground. Finding that fine line is a balance we all must seek and the teachings of the Dalai Lama that I have chosen to include in this book are very much my own lessons in life. And who could argue with the 14th Dalai Lama – except the Chinese government of course.

I have been an active member of the Brisbane Bush Walkers since 2012 and it was here that I learnt many skills as a walker and climber, particularly on longer treks, such as that recounted in *Twenty-One Days in the Himalayas*. BBW has been an active club since 1948, so the skill base is very rich and the people I have come to know there are exceptionally well travelled and skilled in the art of trekking, climbing, and abseiling.

So here is a small list of close friends who I acknowledge directly for their experience and love of wild places – Rod Smith, David Haliczer, Annette Miller, Ray Glancy, David Sydes, Anne Kemp, Chris Hall, Lou and Marion Darveniza – thank you all for your guidance and support over the years.

I also wish to thank Felicity Jodell for her initial editing of the manuscript; Bev Ryan for her professionalism, contacts, and final editing; Jennifer Hall (Jellyfish Creative) for her artistic abilities and final layout – and as a family friend for over forty years. After much consideration I chose IngramSpark to provide the on-demand print service and eBook options – they have been wonderful to work with.

Acknowledgement and appreciation cannot go past the air we breathe, the water we drink, and the food we eat – everything after that is a bonus as we learn to walk this fragile planet with greater gentleness, love, and compassion. It is the direction our human spirit must walk, and it is very interesting to note that the tribal peoples of this planet have known this for 100,000 years or more. Here in Australia, our indigenous peoples have a recorded history and claim to this earth going back at least 60,000 years. They are our true teachers, and I believe the key to our future survival.

TIBETAN PRAYER FLAGS

Traditionally, the five colours are arranged from left to right in a specific order: **blue**, **white**, **red**, **green**, and **yellow**.

The five colours represent the five elements, **Earth**, **Water**, **Fire**, **Air**, and **Space**.

BLUE	symbolizes sky and space
WHITE	symbolizes air and wind
RED	symbolizes fire
GREEN	symbolizes water
YELLOW	symbolizes earth

According to traditional Tibetan medicine, health and harmony are produced through the balance of the five elements. The flags are left in the wind and weather to fall apart and spread their messages of peace and harmony.

FOREWORD

IAN DESCRIBES HIMSELF AS AN ADVENTURER WITH AN ENORMOUS CURIOSITY.
HE HAS HAD A MIXED CAREER AS AN ENGINEER, EDUCATOR AND WRITER, AS WELL AS A VISUAL AND PERFORMING ARTIST.
AN EXTENSIVE TRAVELER, IAN CURRENTLY WORKS AS A GUEST SPEAKER ON CRUISE SHIPS.

The first time I met Tim, we were both stark naked in a sweat lodge. Less than twenty-four hours later we were dancing together, semi-naked.

Before any inappropriate conclusions are drawn, I must add that the dance was the Maori Haka in a session of tribal dance and the occasion was a gathering of men in the Numinbah Valley on the Queensland/New South Wales border. This is a regular event organized by the Men's Wellbeing Association, Qld.

We cemented a bond that weekend which has endured for decades.

Tim's love of life, immense curiosity and a propensity for experiencing life outside of the square, drew me to him. He has been an inspiration to me and to many others.

He has a very real sense of community and has given a large amount of his time and expertise to organizations such as the Men's Wellbeing Association, Qld. Also, his innovative and interesting radio production, "Men's and Women's Stories" for Community Radio was very well received. I had the honour to be an interviewee on one of his earlier productions. He has had an impressive line-up of guests over the last few years and to be a part of it has been a privilege.

A keen bushwalker since a young boy, Tim has trekked in places that most people can only dream about. It was inevitable that he would find himself, eventually, exploring "The Roof of the World", the Himalayas.

I too, have trekked the Himalaya and the vivid images evoked after reading just the first few pages of his story transported me back to the trail and walking through those mystical mountains.

Of course, the photographs are a wonderful supplement to the writing but it is the observations, the details, the experiences and the anecdotes that give life to his visual display.

The reader will encounter a spectacular landscape of immense contrast. A sometimes stark and brutal land which can also be lush, gentle and forgiving. A land of almost overpowering beauty, the sheer majesty of which takes your breath away.

I have found Tim an astute observer of this world, a quality that has always endeared him to me. As he was trekking in the mountains, he describes a people living as an integral part of their environment, not trying to conquer it or tame it but to live in harmony with it. Their temples and statues are but cultural manifestations of their deep spiritual oneness with the land that they share.

Naturally, in the larger towns particularly, the influences of the outside world of the twenty-first century are impacting on traditional culture and beliefs but the landscape is so powerful that the people's spirituality will persevere.

Tim found, as I did, that one had to accept the label of tourist and to be sometimes a source of curiosity when leaving the more frequented routes. We were also a source of income and, as is the situation in most of the world, there were plenty of operators willing to exploit visitors. However, many people who would receive no personal monetary gain from the visitors to their country, were warm, friendly and extremely generous.

Tim is planning to return to Nepal and also, as to his nature, contribute to the community with volunteer work. I wish him well in that endeavour.

To the reader, I say enjoy this book. If you have not already experienced "The Roof of the World", be warned, you will not truly rest until you have.

Ian Stevenson
NOVEMBER, 2018

PROLOGUE

> "LOVE AND COMPASSION ARE NECESSITIES, NOT LUXURIES. WITHOUT THEM HUMANITY CANNOT SURVIVE."
>
> Dalai Lama

I grew up knowing my gran and grandfather, as well as my own parents, very well. I knew my Anglo-Saxon family history and the connections these relationships have within our world.
Our family crest – which has been tattooed on my left shoulder – is both tribal and Anglo-Saxon:

Esto Quod Audes

The translation from Latin simply means to "Be what you dare". However, I prefer a more moderate version of "Be all you can be" – which I encourage my children to strive for. I have not always lived up to that motto in the busyness of life, having been very committed to the raising of my three children and not always able to work fulltime due to an illness that took over ten years to discover and treat. However, this illness was most likely the catalyst to write this story and make it available to the world.

The Nepalese people are a remarkable race that is perhaps 5,000 years old in its current form. China continues to be a threat in a way that Tibet so wrongly experienced some sixty-plus years ago now, and like Tibet, it is unlikely the West would come to the aid of Nepal should the Chinese government choose to spill over their borders – that's code for 'invade'. The enormous concrete and steel bridges I saw being built on the western side of the Annapurna were big enough for semi-trailers to pass over – certainly more than adequate for any tourist flow to the famous Muktinath – but who am I, a humble traveller, to say.

I hope you find inspiration and enjoyment in the text and images included in this book. The Nepalese are a wonderful people that give our planet the uniqueness and diversity that makes life so interesting. I hope we can always help protect their way of life and pray the Himalayas remain the largely unspoilt wilderness it is, as there is nowhere on the planet quite like this landscape and people.

Enjoy, dear reader, and go if the opportunity presents itself.

> "WE ARE VISITORS ON THIS PLANET. WE ARE HERE FOR FOR NINETY OR ONE HUNDRED YEARS AT THE VERY MOST. DURING THIS PERIOD, WE MUST TRY TO DO SOMETHING GOOD, SOMETHING USEFUL WITH OUR LIVES. IF YOU CONTRIBUTE TO OTHER PEOPLE'S HAPPINESS, YOU WILL FIND THE TRUE GOAL, THE TRUE MEANING OF LIFE."

HIS HOLINESS, THE 14TH DALAI LAMA
KOPAN MONASTERY, KATHMANDU

CHAPTER 10

BLUE SYMBOLIZES THE SKY AND SPACE

THORONG LA PASS, 5416 METRES

> "IT ALWAYS SEEMS IMPOSSIBLE UNTIL IT'S DONE."
> Nelson Mandela

My fingertips were stinging in pain – an excruciating, penetrating pain that I could do nothing about – as I stepped oh so slowly forward on an icy surface with my hands holding the hiking poles to help steady me and pull me forward. Because I hadn't brought a Himalayan grade of glove that was adequate in minus fifteen degrees Celsius, no matter how hard I tried to work, my fingers on the trekking poles just stung!

My blood was retracting to the body's core temperature but the nerve endings in my fingers weren't going to allow that, hence the extreme pain! I knew I was doing damage to my fingertips, but I could do nothing but retreat the way we came – or push on to the valley on the other side of the Pass. I had to keep moving forward.

It was a good three-hour trek to Thorong La Pass at 5,416 metres; that's just 3,432 metres below Mt Everest, but anyone who has climbed to these heights knows that is a very big difference. Climbers can lose toes, parts of a foot or hand, a nose and worse depending on the weather and winds, which can howl for three out of four days in winter on the summit of Mt Everest – and many of the other mountains that make up the Himalayas – at over 250kph.

My guide was Akash, a young man of about thirty, and he knew this country very well from the many guided tours he had made here over the years, first as a porter and now in the much more credited role of guide. His English was very good; almost too good in fact, but more on that subject later.

I had started in Pokhara, a very picturesque tourist town nestled into the foothills of the Himalayas, where many such adventures begin. It was the Annapurna Circuit and Base Camps that I had come to experience. And it is the dedicated and experienced climbing teams that can accomplish the very high summits with the blessing of good weather.

LEFT: *Thorong La Pass at 5416 metres*

My twenty-one day trek in comparison to these very high alpine climbs was a walk in the park so to speak; however, the inherent beauty of the Himalayas and the Nepalese/Tibetan culture that has been shared here for thousands of years is nothing but miraculous to say the least. I was here to immerse myself in it for a total of thirty days – which included seven days in Kathmandu, one of the world's most majestic cities in my experience in terms of culture and history.

When Akash and I got to the top of Thorong La Pass we were the first for the day. The altitude is a very real phenomenon to adjust to; my body was working hard to draw oxygen into my muscles, and because of the altitude the oxygen is rarefied. In order to cope the body has to slow down until a balance is reached – a balance of enough oxygen feeding the muscles due to the workload. It was very hard to walk the three hours at a steady climb on the icy, gravelly track that weaved to the summit, not forgetting my stinging and aching finger-tips.

I had started taking Diamox, a Western medication to assist in the acclimatisation process at 3,000 metres, and Akash was insisting I also eat the local brew of garlic soup daily. The most effective method of climbing is to take it slowly and ascend gradually, taking half-day rests wherever possible. This way the body can gradually get used to the rarefied oxygen.

As a way of acclimatising we had trekked out to the famous Tilicho Lake at an elevation of 4,920 metres, the highest lake in the world for its size, which is approximately 4.0km long by 1.2km wide. The climb was hard because of the altitude but the reward was nothing short of extraordinary with the lake's near full coating of ice and another two months of winter coming. But more on Lake Tilicho later.

To give some perspective on the uncertainty of the Himalayas – or any mountains for that matter – in the peak of summer in October 2014, Thorong La Pass received a downfall of 1.8 metres of snow; 43 lives were lost and over 500 people had to be rescued. We were there in early December with some cloud cover, but the weather was quite stable – the gods were favouring us.

Akash didn't want to linger so we took some trekking photos of our success and then made our way down to the very interesting town of Muktinath; a solid four-hour trek on a very reasonable gravel trail, although very steep and not for those with knee problems.

A small village on the way down where we stopped for tea had a group of women who set up a stall selling Yak wool garments featuring many bright colours. They had a timber handloom set up and many scarves, beanies, and legwarmers for sale. I bought a beautiful green scarf for my sister. When it was time to leave I thought about the logistics of their remote location and their ability to die the wool, weave it into a yarn, and then weave it into a scarf, beanie, or legwarmer all using only a small timber handloom. Hmmm? Perhaps these beautiful garments were actually from Kathmandu or Tibet where they had all the sophisticated equipment to produce such fine work.

ABOVE: *Annapurna III looking south from Ledar, 7,555 metres above sea level*
MIDDLE: *Pack horses near Ledar, heading back down to Manang for more supplies to the high country*
RIGHT: *Akash and me at Thorong La Pass, 5,416 metres above sea level*

We stayed the night in Muktinath which looked to be blossoming with tourism as hotels were being built everywhere, and some were very upmarket. Muktinath is a pilgrimage for both Hindus and Buddhists, and Akash led the way up to the entrance where to the west were the Hindu temples and to the east the Buddhist holy places; all very respectful and accepting I thought.

This site was akin to a Muslim and Christian religious site, side by side — but then I don't know of any place like that the world over, but let us not be pedantic. We were in the rarefied climate of the Himalayas, where religion is bound to be more accepting and where modesty is definitely worth embracing, especially if you are humble trekker such as myself. It was these two religions, Hinduism and Buddhism, at this site that people the world over made their pilgrimage to honour.

This place was extraordinary, as research proved. Firstly, we were at an elevation of 3,710 metres and in part of the famous Mustang

Province which borders the infamous – and forbidden to enter – Tibet. My mere mention of our proximity to Tibet and asking if "we could take a side route to the border" left Akash with a glazed look of horror on his face that I should even mention such a thing. I could see "Dumb Westerner," stamped clearly on his forehead, "change the subject now!"

LEFT: *A weaver in a small village near Muktinath*
ABOVE: *The author at the entrance to Muktinath Monastery*
MIDDLE: *The 108 bronze cow heads flowing with icy waters*
RIGHT: *Detail of a bronze cow head*

For thousands of years this place has been sacred to Hindus and Buddhists alike. The name Muktinath literally means 'place of liberation' – hence the attraction for so many pilgrims. It is believed to be the eighth most sacred Hindu shrine and one of the oldest in the world. The Murti, or physical deity, is made of gold and is believed to be the size of a human. Being a foreigner, I was forbidden to enter the shrine, but I could walk around the 108 bronze caste cow heads the size of a cow's hoof that spouted freezing water from a stone wall at almost one metre intervals; devoted male Hindus ran through the spray, and in so doing dramatically reduced their core body temperature. I thought it a very silly ritual at this cold time of year – and the Hindu females seemed to have far more regard for their core body temperature and stayed dry – but I loved seeing the ritual. I love anywhere that is considered sacred on our precious planet. In many ways the sacredness of this place reinforced the sacredness of the planet for the people involved, myself included. (1)

The fact there were 108 of these cow faces was no coincidence. They represent in Hindu philosophy the twelve zodiacs signs times the nine planets, which equals 108. Combined with this are twenty-seven lunar mansions (mansions being a segment of the ecliptic through which the moon passes) with four quarters, which also equals 108 Padas, meaning footprints.

It is the only place on earth where the Hindus and Buddhists celebrate the five elements; fire, water, sky, earth, and air. This is where all the material things of the universe are made according to Hindu and Buddhist tradition. What's more, the enormous Kali Gandaki Nadi River that flowed past Muktinath – and only got bigger as it headed south to the lower regions of Nepal – is believed to have an entire river bed of Shaligram stones which symbolise Vishnu – a principle Hindu deity. I saw many of these stones for sale and was tempted to buy one, not knowing their Hindu meaning at the time. I saw them as black fossilized remains of another time – millions of years old, formed before humankind walked upright.

LEFT: *The Hindu temple of Muktinath*
ABOVE: *The black buddha at the Muktinath Monastery which used to be white only a few years ago*
MIDDLE: *Chinese 'development' on the western side of the Annapurna, near Muktinath*
RIGHT: *The alluvial farming community on Kali Gandaki Nadi river*

What struck me most about this sacred collaboration of Hinduism and Buddhism was the huge black Buddha that rose seven metres high and had a glistening black coating. Akash told me that it was only coated in this way a few years ago; before that it was the natural cream colour of the local stone and blended in too well with the natural landscape from which it had been carved. Maybe a Buddhist committee decided it needed a little oomph from the marketing department to make this beautiful welcome for pilgrims stand out on the horizon for many miles down the valley to the north-west.

Around its rectangular base were eight relief carvings of stylised lions, each unique in appearance; some were cheeky, others quite angry with sharp teeth blazing. All of them suggested to me that this Buddha was not one to mess with, and its new black coat only emphasized this. It is interesting that my research from various sources had no photo of this extraordinary black Buddha, only the creamy coloured one which blended in too well … a good decision by the Buddhist marketing department, I thought.

This was day twelve of our trek, and we were to leave the next day to walk down the mighty Kali Gandaki Nadi River to Jomsom, another major tourist town with its own airport for pilgrims to fly to, but I did wonder if the airport would serve for other intentions – perhaps in ten or more years' time with the burgeoning red dragon to the north-east – God forbid!

As striking as this enormous river was, which in places must have been several kilometres across, it was very obvious – in view of the third major bridge under construction – that the Chinese were investing large amounts of money into this region. As a Westerner looking at such projects, it is very hard to believe that this massive investment in infrastructure was to help the local Nepalese and was not, in fact, more for the benefit of China. What's more, it's very obvious that with Tibet now under Chinese rule (since 1959) this proposed road could in fact be heading right over the top and into Tibet. That could mean McDonald's at Thorong La Pass, with the token Tibetan flags for the tourists flying from the golden arches – God forbid!

But why are the Chinese investing so much into this region with Tibet so close? I doubt it is to visit the magnificent black Buddha. Perhaps one only needs to be grateful they don't bulldoze over it in a sure sign of expansionism; it certainly feels that way already with the massive bridges and the illustrious Tibet just a stones' throw away, so to speak. All I can say is God help the Annapurna Circuit and the thousands of villagers who make a very good living from Western trekkers like myself.

Perhaps the future is more about bus tours – McDonald's at the pass before shooting through to Tibet and down to Lhasa for a quick gamble on the two Chinese state-owned lotteries; one for sport and one for charity, ho! ho! ho! Now this sounds like a complete blob of nonsense to me and a front for more serious gambling operations; state-owned lotteries indeed! (2)

But where does my cynicism come from regarding the Chinese? It could be their expansionist history going back several thousand years – can't argue with that! Or is it their love of hardball gambling? Can't argue with that, either! Thank God I live in Australia and can write such things with no one giving too much of a toss for my opinion! Perhaps it's China's woeful human rights record, or known jailings – and in many cases murder – of journalists who dare to cross the party line. I'll stop this right here! I am a humble trekker experiencing the wonder of the Himalayas, and too pretty for a Chinese jail!

For now there are no bitumen roads, just really rough four wheel drive tracks that can take one all the way to Jomsom, where the affluent traveller can catch a twin Otter plane back to Kathmandu. Or perhaps a Hercules C-130 military supply plane could be landed there from Beijing?

There is already a military base in Jomsom, right in the middle of town, with accommodation for a thousand or more men. The Nepalese Jomsom Military Base could easily be transformed into a Chinese Jomsom Military Base with the landing of one Hercules. The rest of the world probably wouldn't do too much at all no matter how loud the trekkers complained; somewhat akin to what they did with Tibet. We screamed and yelled in the safety of the West, but nothing really changed for the Tibetans who did stay on their land, many of whom are still persecuted to this day. One very sure fact is the Fourteenth Dalai Lama of Tibet is not returning soon ... even for a holiday.

We trekked this beautiful and massive river system all the way to Jomsom; it was by far the biggest river system I had ever seen in my life. As for the Chinese, they possibly have plans for the world's largest hydroelectric project, with the proceeds heading over the Himalayas into Tibet to drive the massive mining projects they are planning on the Tibetan Plateau.

I trailed behind Akash for one hundred metres or more as I photographed this incredible river system, with villages built out over massive rock scree deltas. No matter how big the road was going to be, the Chinese will never destroy this ancient geological grandeur or the villagers that have lived and farmed here for thousands of years. May the gods bless the Himalayan people! May they stay with their traditional ways and not be sucked into the void of McDonald's golden arches, and Chinese expansionism.

Jomsom was a busy hub of tourist hotels, most waiting for the high seasons of April and October. The airstrip hummed with twin engine aircraft, and we passed the very large army base with its own rock-climbing training cliffs right in the middle of town. I assumed – and hoped – it was the Nepalese Army. Construction of large bitumen highways only a few years away from completion were happening before my eyes.

But why would the Chinese invade? I mean expand – a more diplomatic term! China's population sits at 1.403 billion, give or take a few million and, let's face it, Nepal has lots of water which can be used to run hydroelectric plants, while Tibet is rich in minerals – even uranium – so Nepal could well have the same geological make-up. And let's not forget the vast food bowl that is the Himalayas, and the very resourceful people who farm it. (3)

So why would the Chinese invade – I mean expand? Because they can! And no nation is ever going to challenge them even though it is morally wrong, just like it was morally wrong when they crushed Tibet and robbed her of her spiritual presence back in 1959. There's been little in the way of counterattack from Tibet in the past fifty-nine years, except for Buddhist monks that take their lives by self-immolation. The count for these desperate acts

LEFT: *Kali Gandaki Nadi river, looking south-west*
ABOVE: *Suspension bridge heading to Jomsom*
MIDDLE: *Chillies drying in the winter sun, Tatopani*
RIGHT: *My new friends at the Tatopani hot, hot and very hot springs*

of defiance over these fifty-nine years is not clear, but certainly since February of 2009, 151 male and female Tibetan monks have surrendered their lives, and since December 2017 a further 152 have lost their lives in violent protest, but it seems there are most likely many more than this. At least 10 have been in exile, including those at Kathmandu's Boudhanath Stupa, where tens of thousands of Western tourists go every year, but nothing has changed in terms of China's dragon grip. (4)

For the Chinese military police in Tibet those desperate acts of protest are nothing more than a mess to clean up on the pavement – they do not care! Tibet belongs to China in their expansionist eyes, and for a lot more reasons than we in the West care to comfortably understand. It is also evident that the Chinese authorities have censored much material from the country that

was Tibet, and the 14th Dalai Lama still resides in Northern India for fear of his life. In 1989 he won the Nobel Peace Prize, and to this day works tirelessly in support of his Tibetan people.

If he decided to take a little summer break and return to Tibet, he would be arrested by the Chinese police and thrown in jail until the world kicked up enough of a fuss that even the Chinese couldn't ignore. It seems rather odd to me that an extraordinary man like the 14th Dalai Lama could be jailed in his own country; he was, after all, born there and is the rightful heir to the position he holds today, which goes back to at least the thirteenth century. Try explaining that to the Chinese authorities and you'd be thrown in jail too, just for speaking his name! God knows what would happen if you tried to take him a fresh set of clothes! (5)

On Day 14, we took a bus ride from Jomsom down to Tatopani. Now when I say 'bus ride', I must make clear that there is NOTHING in those two words that could be considered even slightly fun or pleasant or enjoyable or even restful. Firstly, the mechanics must have welded the suspension leaves together, taken out the shock absorbers, and made sure every seat spring had been welded rigid. After ten kilometres of this bouncing, tormenting experience I had concluded my buttocks were also now welded rigidly; there seemed to be no give whatsoever in this bus, or in my body for that matter.

Then, to top it off, I was convinced the Chinese road builders had made preparations for Day 14 of Tim Easton's trek – that 'Western dog!' – to ensure that I would be bounced around so ferociously for a generous six hours or more that I would never write again ... especially about expansionist China!

My dear guide must have bribed the man sitting in the middle of the bus to move over so I could have some Western comfort because, as luck would have it, I drew the very rear seat where – after the first ten kilometres or so – my body was almost reduced to human jelly, and not a pleasant flavour I can assure you. Sort of bright red in colour with way too many white bony bits to make it worth eating.

At various times I did manage to put my head towards the window and catch glimpses of the magnificent Kali Gandaki Nadi River, but with my body having been so shaken about, it resembled more of a blurred vision of white frothy water and grey rock. I did however see three of the large concrete bridge structures the Chinese were financing. I could almost see the mounting brackets for the Red Star flag of imperialist China, but I'm sure that was nothing more than my brain and eyesight being turned to mush by the 'road'. The Chinese love their neighbours; there is proof of that just across the border in Tibet and now sixty-eight years on, their invasion continues.

PREVIOUS PAGE: *The waters are healing and beautifully relaxing after 'a bus ride to die for', Tatopani*
ABOVE: *Nilgiri South, 6,839 metres above sea level from Tatopani township*
MIDDLE: *Kali Gandaki Nadi river*
RIGHT: *Legumes drying in Tatopani*

Our destination, Tatopani, is a heaven on earth, not just because of the beautiful hotel we stayed in – which had friendly staff and a lovely, well tended garden – but also because the mountains were not far away. I took countless photos of the outline of Nilgiri (South), a 6,839 metre mountain of such dramatic proportions that I had to keep looking and checking to see that it was real and not just painted on the town's backdrop to amuse the tourists.

There were just a few of us tourists in town, including the South Korean family who had been following us from Manang and with whom I tried to spark up a conversation on several occasions to get their thoughts on North Korea and those very big rockets they had been sending off to various parts of the Sea of Japan. However, they just wanted to trek and talk trekking gear, or places they had trekked all over the world ... anything but politics, thank you! I learnt to submit to their friendly avoidance system; hell, the South Koreans have been doing that for over sixty years, and you can't blame them when they have such a challenging neighbour.

It was not until I got to Annapurna Base Camp on Day 18 that I discovered how much the Koreans loved to climb mountains. There were memorials in nearly every direction to the lost or fallen on Annapurna, and the climbing museum in Pokhara abounded with information about Korean expeditions, both successful and some not so. They are a very able race, both physically and also strategically. They obviously apply that philosophy to their economy too.

ABOVE: *A very beautiful Tibetan woman, Tatopani*
MIDDLE: *Meat drying on the roof tops*
RIGHT: *Vegetables drying in the winter sun and wind*
FAR RIGHT: *Eager English learners, at my service – please!*

The other wonderful things about Tatopani were the hot springs which flowed just next to that majestic river – the Kali Gandaki Nadi. At this point the river was quite narrow and very, very fast. I trotted down from the hotel with my towel over my shoulder. There were very few tourists and a dozen or so Nepalese who came to bathe in these healing waters, which are between 42 and 48 degrees Celsius. One must know when it's time to step out, as the possibility of becoming a 'boiled lobster' was in fact very real. After that shake up in the bus I possibly resembled something of a lobster but the Indian family who befriended me insisted on a group photo with me centre stage; it was very lovely to be part of such a family photo. I could only wonder what they told their friends back home: "Now this bloke was from Australia – his skin was pink and boiled like a lobster from the hot springs". I spent most of the morning soaking up these medicinal waters, and my body certainly felt very nurtured and soothed by the process.

In the afternoon I walked the length of the small village, which was built around tourism. It was no surprise that the shops were tasteful and had a focus on Tibetan goods. At one point I looked down over a building site (an occupational hazard of mine); I just loved to watch the men and women preparing concrete. One man was building a circular stone staircase for the interior of the hotel lobby, I guessed. Others prepared the timber shutters and then stood them against the reinforcement, which is no different to what we use in Australia.

I made many such observations on my travels, mostly of hotels for tourists, and found that these people know how to build – just don't mention the plumbing, which mostly seems to spray in all directions. And the electricity ... well that's another story which would require great explanation, but I'm fairly sure most of it is sourced in the Himalayas, and comes from smaller hydro plants – and the lights do work most of the time.

LEFT: *Grandmother wisdom*
ABOVE: *A mother with her baby girl - so blessed to be 2018 - twenty years ago her baby could have been sold off to slavery in India*
MIDDLE: *Fresh beans and vitality*
RIGHT: *Healthy Himalayan chicken*

At this particular building site I observed a grandad with his grandson – together they watched the work in progress below as only a grandad and grandson can do together the world over. I do hope my children are reading this as I did feel a certain warmth from this global phenomenon ... now there's no rush kids; dad has many more adventures to complete before I am ready to watch the workings of a building site with my own grandson, but I will be there for that grand occasion – guaranteed!

Another few hundred metres along the town promenade were two women in their late thirties I guessed, with two young children around ages eight and ten. I asked if they would mind me taking a photograph – I always asked (especially the women) regarding photographs, as they must get inundated with requests in peak tourist time. One of the women was particularly photogenic; she had the most striking features, and I guessed she was of Tibetan origin. Their English was far better than my Nepalese and before I knew it, the children were hurried off to get their homework books.

I was rather touched to be the default English teacher as the children and I worked through the spelling of the written words of English; "but, the, today, how, my name is, help, to ..." and then the pronunciation. These children were very quick to catch on;

RIGHT: *Garlic fields which are an excellent food source for altitude sickness according to the locals – I still used Diamox from 3,000 metres*

I wanted to visit the school and help out, but I was told it was currently closed for holiday time. However, it was so good to see two eager learners. I hope and pray they go on to become diplomatic negotiators for Nepal.

I walked on to the end of the town and then followed the river along to the stone staircase that took me up to my hotel. Goodness knows where Akash was, but I suspected he certainly needed a day off from me. I realised I had made a mistake hiring Akash for the whole twenty-one days; it was certainly nothing to do with him – he was a very good guide. It was more that I needed the freedom to do exactly as I wanted instead of being shown and ordered around; put your pack here, this is your room, dinner is at 7.00pm, brush your teeth before you go to bed. He was just doing his job, but it did not sit well with my independence.

What's more, one would have to try very hard to get lost on the Annapurna with its formed trails and stone staircases in many areas. Maps at 1:100,000 were available; not the best scale but sufficient. Many of the locals, especially those in the Himalayas, could speak good English and could cook a fine pizza, poach eggs on toast, and brew a pretty good coffee without the $5,000 coffee machines we have in the West. But I did not know this, even with all my preparations and the help from friends who had done trips similar to mine. For me, it was also something important to assist in the lives of those that I came in contact with, and Akash was one such person. My leaning towards helping the owners of hotels and tea houses, however, became more of a priority than helping Akash with his Ray-Ban sunglasses and developing arrogance.

By the time we got to Ghorepani – a full day's hike through open forest filled with Nepalese oak trees, bamboo, and rhododendrons – relations were becoming strained between us. It was Day 15, and I tried to explain that I really needed to finish the last six days on my own. I don't know if he took offence to that – perhaps he thought I was essentially sacking him, which I most certainly wasn't. He was a very competent young man, but perhaps he feared he would lose part of his payment from his boss in Kathmandu. I did not know and, unfortunately, there was too much machismo around his guiding position to really talk this through. I wished there was a neutral third party available to help discuss this properly – but alas there wasn't – and perhaps loss of face for Akash was very real.

He tried at one point, when we had turned into the valley that heads up to Annapurna Base Camp, to sit me down and spell out the 'anguish' I had been causing him over the past ten days. I didn't realise I was getting a trekkers' report card. He began to tell me of all the woe I had brought him, writing down each woe in a fashion of blame and control. I stood up and just cut to the chase, telling him we had to finish the job ... but that meant another five days together, and something had to give before then – I was sure of that!

ABOVE: *One of the many leafy green healthy vegetables that flourish in these lands*

MIDDLE: *The author in the Rhododendron forests near Ghorepani*

RIGHT: *I think this is the same vegetable put through a press, then added to soups – delicious!*

I would try to call his boss, but this was difficult in these mountainous parts to say the least. I did get through at one point, but he was insistent that we needed to finish this and I agreed very reluctantly. There had been another very low point just before Tadapani when we had walked into a small village and he called out something to the locals which I was very certain was derogatory towards me – the Westerner who couldn't speak Nepalese. This had happened several times before and it was the people's reaction that convinced me something was out of order here, so I decided to confront him; however, my timing was not the best as we were in the middle of nowhere with nil tourist support.

I removed his Ray-Ban sunglasses, looked deep into his dark brown eyes, and challenged him over his "name calling". Ooops! Before I knew it he had his pack and shirt off. He was ready for a "biff", as he called it. I had overstepped the mark, but I wasn't going to put up with what was essentially bullying. Fortunately, he realised he had overstepped the mark too, and I just kept saying to him that we needed to get to Tadapani, which was only an hour away, and talk to his boss back in Kathmandu – easier said than done!

His shirt and pack went back on and we proceeded to Tadapani. I was now determined to be rid of him. We had lunch – separately I might add – but there was no phone reception, so we proceeded further up the valley. This was possibly a huge mistake, as our relationship had moved to a new low. On the next leg of the trek it was very up and down, with long sections of stone stairs. At one point he was following me so close that he was in danger of tripping me up, which could have had dire consequences for me – not him!

The last five days of this trek were going to be mine, and mine alone. Never would I enter into such a guiding agreement again; instead, I would hire someone local for the challenging parts.

About an hour after leaving Tadapani, with lunch having settled in my digestive system, I began to feel stomach cramps; not enough to roll over and die, but certainly causing me great discomfort. I had heard stories of troublesome tourists being fed bicarbonate of soda to send them on their way. The more I thought about it, the more possible it seemed as Akash clearly had some bullying issues in his repertoire of "shadow self" – his removal of his shirt and sounding like a 'snorting bull' was really the last straw for me! The bi-carb was just a discomfort that spelled even louder that our days of guide/tourist trekker were over! It was possible it was simply some stomach upset from the food or water, but that was unlikely as I had been in the Himalayas over two weeks now and this was the first intestinal discomfort I had experienced.

It seemed ironic to me that here we were, in one of the most beautiful parts of the world, and we were bickering like children. It was during this stretch in the oak forests that we came across several families of Grey Langur monkeys. They were quite large – similar in size to a wallaby – grey in colour with a white frill around their black faces. As they moved through the bush they banged and crashed like a herd of elephants, but they were a beautiful sight.

We were to stop in Sinuwa for the night, arriving about 4.00pm, which provided plenty of time to relax and wander about the farming land. We were at Day 15. It was here that Akash decided

LEFT: *Annapurna South from Poon Hill*

he wanted to talk to me again, and he herded me into the small dining hall for 'interrogation'. I listened for about two minutes to his whining about the 'bad Westerner'. If the table had not been screwed down, I may well have lifted it up and over him – there were two people in this mess!

Instead I just said repeatedly that we had to stick to the plan and finish the job like his boss had said. My real plan, however, was to get rid of him at whatever cost, and as soon as possible.

On the outer side of this dining hall was an enormous mud nest that the owner told me was a Himalayan bee nest. I had read about these large bees – the largest in the world, in fact. At 20mm long they were not something to invite for dinner or catch in your hair. Just the sight of them landing on the nest was enough to spell out a warning. The guesthouse owner explained, in his broken English, that it was bad luck to remove them which is easy to understand: who in their right mind would voluntarily take on that job?

Twelve months prior to this trip I had read about the brave Nepalese men and women who hunt for bee nests in the Himalayas, and risk life and limb to retrieve the honey. It seems the Himalayan bee doesn't like to just hand over the merchandise, but then bees the world over generally don't just give it up. (6) Perhaps our native Australian bee – barely five millimetres in length – is the least resistant, but then it is hardly built to defend and its honey production is minimal compared to the larger European bees.

With some research I discovered it was in fact a Himalayan mud wasp, with the nest glued to this man's dining hall. This wasp was forty millimetres in length and landed and took off like a Harrier jet; and something to stay well clear of. The nest really did make a wonderful decoration on the side of his dining hall even if it obscured much of the view, being nearly five soccer balls in size. What happens when the nest completely takes over the dining hall is anyone's guess! However, it would probably become a tourist attraction in itself; I just hope the guesthouse owner is not caught permanently in the nest with only a snorkel for air.

> "WE ARE ALL VISITORS TO THIS TIME, THIS PLACE. WE ARE JUST PASSING THROUGH. OUR PURPOSE HERE IS TO OBSERVE, TO LEARN, TO GROW, TO LOVE…AND THEN WE RETURN HOME."

INDIGENOUS AUSTRALIAN PROVERB

CHAPTER 02

WHITE SYMBOLIZES THE AIR AND WIND

MACHHAPUCHHRE BASE CAMP, 3700 METRES

Helen Keller

At the next opportunity, on Day 15, I called Akash's boss and did manage to get through, but he was adamant that he wanted to see us finish, and perhaps that was something to do with the way the payment system worked. Kewal was Akash's boss based in Kathmandu who I describe in more detail further into the story – he was a very intelligent young entrepreneur who had been a porter and built his business on the trekking trade. He was not interested in the politics of our journey. He just wanted a smooth transition and landing for our trek – and all would then be good in his eyes – but he was not here experiencing what Akash and I were going through. The cultural differences were pulling us apart and it seemed no amount of good humour or 'niceties' could keep us together. Too much had happened and I needed some time alone in these special mountains.

We made it to Dovan that night, just a day's walk to Machhapuchhre Base Camp. There was a very steady set of stone stairs behind us and ahead of us; it was really quite a test physically, but I just loved it. My body was responding so well to the physical challenges, even after sixteen days. Akash had complimented me several times on this trek that I walked like a man in my twenties; I really was quite chuffed by that, and I had enjoyed his company for ninety percent of the trip.

Maybe we would have remained friends throughout a trek if I had not hired him for all of the twenty-one days. However, when he came to serve me at the dinner table that night (a process I hated at the best of times) as if I was the British Royalty and he was the suppressed colonial Nepalese worker from five generations ago I was most uncomfortable. I was sitting next to a Canadian couple and they knew all too well that things were not good between Akash and I. We really needed to part company, and the sooner the better, with all due respect.

LEFT: *Pack horses working hard carrying building materials and tourist supplies, near Chomrong*

The gods were with us in the morning. Akash knocked on my door to say he was leaving. I didn't even open the door, I just wished him well. One of the things I found most challenging with Akash was his concern that I would find out from other Westerners what the local rates were for food and accommodation. I was certainly paying more, but I accepted this as part of the package that came with his guiding services.

What I did find challenging though was all the little extras that came along on a daily basis which, in some cases, added up to an extra US$10/day. It was not an all-inclusive package by any means; things like hot water, drinking water, firewood, Wi-Fi, and hot and cold drinks were all extra in many places. I found myself keeping a close check on these "extras" as I was very sure whose pocket the money was going into. I was waiting for oxygen to be an extra; we were after all trekking through rarefied air! And this type of air does not come cheap!

In the overall scheme of things, it was not really much, but it was all part of me not feeling in control of my trek and especially of my finances. I had paid for an inclusive package back in Kathmandu – something I would never do again however good I thought it was for the Nepalese economy. I was more interested in keeping my own economy in check, and also having the freedom to trek with other Westerners and share their stories. This experience was way too controlled with Akash at the helm.

I thought about writing to the Nepalese tourist authority, the Australian Embassy in Nepal, and even the Lonely Planet guidebook blogs to explain the dangers of this type of tourist package, but then for some Western travellers maybe this was exactly what they wanted. When I reached Pokhara, where there was ample Wi-Fi, I did write to Lonely Planet, but it has been over two months and I haven't heard back from them. I found plenty of stories on their website though, warning trekkers of these tourist packages. They are not necessarily bad; they just don't suit everybody. Hello! Lesson learnt! There were many stories, particularly of Western women travelling alone with Nepalese male guides and being sexually harassed on an almost daily basis. A very big stick might be useful in such cases!

Fortunately, Nepalese female guides are becoming a reality now, and I bet that took years of gender negotiating. This culture – and Akash was no exception – is misogynous. I did meet one

Nepalese woman learning the ropes to become a guide. I hope many more follow in her footsteps so Western women can travel safely on their own here.

It is a sad fact in Nepalese society that when girls have been born, some have been sold off into virtual slavery. Many end up in Indian brothels and if they return home pregnant, they are often shunned by their own family. Thankfully, an organisation was set up in 2000 called The Nepal Youth Foundation, which came up with a novel offer to families with baby girls. They give the family a piglet and kerosene stocks for every baby girl who is kept in the family. The organisation also pays for her to be educated. (7)

ABOVE: *A Gurkha tap in one of the many villages that were so fortunate to have this army service*
MIDDLE: *The terraced fields being prepared for the winter crops or to wait till next Spring, near Chomrong*
RIGHT: *Potatoes, nearly ready for digging at Sinuwa*

It seems remarkable that a piglet and some kerosene can be used to dramatically change the course of a little girl's life while boys are treated vastly different; women who give birth to a son are held in high regard, but not so if they give birth to a girl. It is estimated from rural and impoverished areas that some 10,000 to 15,000 girls are tricked or sold into slavery either as domestic, factory, or sex workers every year. It is also estimated that over 100,000 Nepali women currently work in Indian brothels. (8)

But I do have to say – without having read the research – that I found Nepalese women to be empowered, or at least that is how it appeared. In many places they ran the guesthouse or tea shop or gift shop or restaurant, and they were very lively characters. However, I did read that Himalayan women were the exception within Nepal.

I left Dovan that morning heading north-east to Machhapuchhre feeling a mixture of things. I was greatly relieved that Akash had

LEFT: *The rhododendron and oak forests of the Annapurna, near Ghandruk*

gone home, but the fear of reprisal was very strong in my mind and, let's face it, if he wanted to arrange an 'accident' he could. I remained vigilant, especially on the sections of the trail where there were no people. I was very aware of the hundred metre drops to the icy Modi Khola River below; I couldn't afford to be going on, playing the 'amazed tourist' I certainly had been. I needed to get a firm grip on these possibilities – however, being paranoid wasn't helpful or necessary; I just had to keep a mindful eye on the remote situation I was in, and beware of an ex-guide heading for home.

It was a huge climb up to the base of 'Fish Tail', as the mountain is affectionately nicknamed, and one view from this north-east approach makes this name very clear. The peak of the mountain looks like a fish's tail diving back into the water. The Nepalese government forbids it to be climbed, as it is believed to be of particular significance to the deity Shiva, the principle deity of Hinduism. "Shiva is the destroyer of evil and the transformer." "Shiva is the Supreme being who creates, protects and transforms the universe." (9) I needed some of that as I ventured forward! The mountain's official name is Machhapuchhre, and it stands at 6,997 metres.

I arrived at the base camp mid-afternoon and checked into a modest guesthouse just at the base of the summit. One of the problems I now faced with Akash gone was that he left me with no Nepalese cash. I was still four day's trek from Pokhara, and there were no ATM machines until I got there. I would need to rely on some kind tourist to lend me the money; approximately US$50 would feed, shelter, and buy me a jeep ride to civilisation. It was fortunate that I bumped into John and Sara, the Canadian couple who heard firsthand the strained relations between Akash and myself – and they had also witnessed the colonial antics of him serving me dinner, a nonsensical charade if there ever was one. Perhaps it was because of my British heritage – I've had it pointed out before – but it's not who I am.

John and Sara were staying in the much bigger accommodation complex above where I was. I went to have afternoon tea there with the remaining rupees I was carrying and they very generously offered to lend me the US$50 which would get me to Pokhara. I was over the moon; it felt like Shiva was looking after me and that I had somehow triumphed over adversity. I walked back to my accommodation to order dinner and settle in for a

RIGHT: *The author at Annapurna Base Camp*

cosy night as the temperature was dropping fast. We were at 3,700 metres, it was gently snowing, and it was Christmas Eve with no family to celebrate with, but I really did not care. I just loved being here on my own amongst these extraordinary mountains.

Most of the tourists were staying at the higher residences – perhaps fifty trekkers in total – but in peak tourist times this combined complex catered for several hundred guests at least. The horse teams that service these hotels must work seven days per week bringing up food and other supplies for this mega tourist trade. Thank God I had chosen to come when I did, as I don't enjoy large groups – all clambering for the next great photo. Of course, I was doing exactly the same, but at least I could 'pretend' I was here on my own exploring one of the world's great natural beauties – the Himalayas.

The next day was Christmas, and I was up early to spend the day at South Annapurna Base Camp, a steady two hour climb to a set of hotels that catered for at least another two hundred people in the high season. Fortunately, I counted only about twelve other travellers and maybe ten staff to operate the teahouses. We were now at an elevation of 4,130 metres with Annapurna I rising to 8,091 metres just a short distance up the valley and across massive glaciers some ten kilometres long and about six kilometres wide.

I walked up to the hundreds of flags that decorated the many memorials of fallen or lost climbers, many of whom were from Korea. I didn't realise just what a climbing nation they were until this trip, and seeing the Korean family that followed us for much of the first leg I realized that they were indeed very capable trekkers. One very elaborate memorial was to a Korean woman and several of her team who had perished only a few years ago when the weather turned for the worse. This climbing team also got a strong mention in the International Mountaineering Museum in Pokhara.

As the watery sun rose ever so slightly on the northern horizon it was very pleasant to just lounge around on the few grassy knolls that remained, as snow now mostly covered them. About every two hours a helicopter would buzz up the valley from Pokhara, drop off half a dozen passengers, and take the previous group back down. These people did a two hour tour of the Himalayas – or at least this section of it – took their photos, had a cup of tea in the teahouse, and headed back to the tourist lights of Pokhara. This is perhaps good for the Nepalese economy, but I have to be honest – a roaring helicopter in these wild, mountainous places,

LEFT: *Memorial to a Korean woman, Ji Hyeon-Ok, a climber who died on Annapurna I in 1999, Annapurna Base Camp*

unless doing a medical evacuation, just seems out of place to me. There is serenity to be found here without the buzzing of flying machines in my opinion.

Not my cup of tea at all! In fact, their annoying buzz up the valley made me wish for low cloud cover, but that was perhaps a little unsporting of me. Perhaps they were collecting data for their next real estate venture: condos on the side of the fishtail! There would just be the odd incentive needed to smooth over the Shiva issue. Hah! As if Shiva would allow that; she certainly had proven her presence and support for me in the form of the delightful Canadian couple who came to my financial and, in some ways, emotional rescue.

Of particular interest was the memorial to Chris Bonington, the British mountaineer who, in 1970, climbed Annapurna I in what was described as the greatest achievement of modern mountaineering. He pioneered a new and bolder approach to high altitude climbing, and while one of his party died in an avalanche, one can only marvel at such feats of physical, emotional, and mental endurance. (10)

There is an excellent documentary film by John Edwards; what I found most interesting about this short film was the "coolness" of the men, their humbleness and respect for the mountains. (11) There was no ego; they were well aware the mountain could crush and kill them at any moment. They also showed no rush to complete the task, accepting that their safety was more important than getting to the top. It was also interesting to see their gear up close – not much different from what we use now. They were a party of eleven climbers of great courage, and let's not forget the hundreds of Sherpas hired for the job of lifting supplies to 6,000 metres and more.

The Sherpas were retired Gurkhas who wanted to earn the four pounds per week on offer. None of them had ever been to the height of base camp three before, which was just over 6,000 metres, where five tonnes of provisions had to be carried. There were four hundred Sherpas hired who traditionally accepted the mountains as the "dwelling places of the gods". The expedition was up against early monsoonal weather and it took them six weeks to reach just under 7,000 metres, but on 27 May 1970 at 14.30 hours one of the men reached the summit. Regrettably, three days later on descent, Ian Clough was killed by a massive avalanche; the ice chunk was as big as a house and this set the tone for the remainder of the expedition. It is not hard to see why true climbers are humble people – death is always close.

They buried Ian Clough at the Annapurna Base Camp; a small grave at the foot of the rocks he had trained the Sherpas on. Chris Bonington describes the risk of climbing as inevitable, as tragic as it was. It was obvious to see the respect the Sherpas had for Ian in the documentary. I fit squarely with the Nepalese – these mountains connect with me spiritually and while it is very inspiring and important to visit them and draw from their strength, that is where I draw the line. That is what I need – a spiritual connection with the earth and universe, and it is possible to find that here. It starts for me by accepting and being quiet about my business; only in this way can I begin to hear our silent heartbeat and that of the Planet.

Another significant display in the International Mountaineering Museum in Pokhara shows the amount of climbing rubbish that continues to be a problem on Mt Everest particularly, which has been climbed since the 1920s. The British were the first, but it wasn't until 1953 that Sir Edmund Hillary and Tenzing Norgay, using oxygen, "knocked the 8,848 metres off!" There were years of media speculation as to whose foot actually got there first. Hello, as if it's even important considering the five hundred or more men and women who were the back-up team that made their achievement possible ... whose foot got there first? No wonder the gods shudder at us at times! (12)

The museum had a truckload of gas bottles, ice stakes, ropes of both steel and nylon, water bottles, and tent remains, to name a few items. Mt Everest is rapidly becoming a climber's landfill, and is perhaps losing its spiritual mystery, with homo sapiens climbing all over it for a Facebook photo. When will we grow beyond this limited view of the Earth – and the Universe for that matter? Of course, this would mean we would have to accept our frailty and become a part of the natural order of things, somewhat akin to the traditional peoples of this world who have believed and understood this for thousands of years. The traditional peoples had no need to conquer anything – they knew their place and accepted it with the greatest of wisdom and humility. What's more, they practiced a natural order of sustainability that didn't require climbing the highest mountain on the Planet. No need! They knew who they were - sometimes a more difficult pursuit in the West, where the pressure to perform on the economic growth curve can crush who we are as individuals.

It is estimated over 290 people have died trying to climb Mt Everest. It is not known how many of these were Nepalese porters, but in the very first British expedition of 1922, nine were killed. More than 4,000 people have scaled the summit since Sir Edmund Hilary and Tenzing Norgay first climbed the mountain in 1953. Nepalese porters are an integral part of the hard and dangerous slog required to get supplies to the seven or more camps needed for such a climb. (13)

In April 2015 at least eighteen Nepalese porters were killed in a huge avalanche as they were carrying Westerners' supplies up to one of the camps. An excellent film called *Sherpa* by Australian film maker Jennifer Peedom questioned this Western need for a Facebook photo when so many Nepalese lives had been lost. The usual argument ensued about creating income and wealth and opportunities for those porters, who would otherwise be 'poor' farmers, but that is how they have lived for thousands of years. Who are we to impose some new grand vision upon their lives when so many are 'killed in action' so to speak? And for what? A Facebook moment? We in the West have so much to learn from these people.

The Nepalese Sherpas — who are drawn to the big money of Western tourists who pay upward of US$70,000 to climb Mt Everest — were caught in an avalanche as they carried supplies up to Western base camps with loads of almost 70kg, their own body weight being around 57kg. The Western tourists' aim, in many cases, is to put their 'achievement' on Facebook — I just don't get it — and they carry a minimal of equipment, food, clothing, tents, and sleeping gear, to name just a few necessary items needed for such a challenging climb.

I was searching for a more spiritual journey and appreciation for the magnificence of these mountains at a safer 4,130 metres, where the probability of being seriously injured or killed in an avalanche or losing fingers, toes, and possibly a nose through frostbite in areas where temperatures can plummet to minus forty, depending on the wind speed, is greatly reduced. To me this possibility is just not fun, however good I would look on Facebook — and the number of likes I may or may not get! I question our motivation in the West when these climbs are made available for anyone with the required US$70k. I think we in the West could do

LEFT: *Machhapuchhre (or 'Fish Tail') 6,997 metres above sea level*

with a lot more spiritual awareness of this precious planet, and that would come from listening more to the East, and of course our own Indigenous people here in Australia.

Climbers talk about the 'death zone' – which is around the 8,000 metre mark, where oxygen is used faster than it can be replenished. The need to carry oxygen is often essential and these are large bottles of about ten litres. While I am sure many climbing parties aim to bring their used gear back down with them, it only takes a small shift in the weather for that good intention to go completely out the door; hence the rubbish problem that still exists on Mt Everest – not forgetting the dead bodies that now line the route.

EcoHimal was established in 1992 and, among other things, they run ongoing clean up campaigns on Mt Everest and other places in the Himalayas. Their goals are as follows: "The fight against poverty and the protection of biodiversity in order to guarantee the long-term sensible coexistence of man and nature – these are the major tasks of any development cooperation." (14) I would add some spiritual training for the Westerners who intend to climb to the big heights aided by the Nepalese Sherpas at US$70,000 per person; there is a discount for couples! That would fund a lot of clean-up operations including sewerage, removal of dead bodies, and climbers' waste, to name a few.

Since EcoHimal started clean-up operations on and around Everest they have removed twenty-five tonnes of rubbish; twelve thousand kilograms of paper and plastic, and over eleven tonnes of human waste. The Nepalese government now charges each climbing expedition US$4,000 as a deposit to make these groups responsible for their own rubbish removal, no matter what the weather.

The seven hundred climbers and support teams that make the climb every season have resulted in "traffic jams" near the summit of Mt Everest, waiting for their own moment of glory to stand on the summit of the world – I personally just don't get it! I am a Westerner and someone who loves the mountains, but I do not understand this need to 'conquer mountains' when it has certainly been my experience that there is a great deal to conquer within: human relationships, world peace, and weapon disarmament sit fairly high on my list! *But let's head off and conquer Mt Everest instead, then we won't have to think about such tricky topics and, while we are there, let's throw our rubbish around for someone else to clean up.* Our behaviour just hasn't been very responsible and the Nepalese way of life could have continued well without our Western influence – but that was never going to happen.

On a lighter note, many organisations are doing great work to combat the poo factor by utilizing a clever biogas system located at Everest Base Camp, but what happens after this camp is anyone's guess! In ideal conditions it takes five to seven days to climb Mt Everest; now multiply one poo per day by twelve in a party of climbers ... that's a fair bit of poo for just one group, and there are an estimated seven hundred climbers per year. That doesn't include the back-up crews of Sherpas. You can do the math! It's just too scary! Mt Everest, for all its magnificence, may need to be re-named the Human Poo and Climbing Rubbish Mountain of the planet! It really doesn't have the same ring about it. May the Gods intervene in this dilemma!

I headed back down to my guesthouse, stopping for tea at the more touristy venue. I ended up talking with a Russian filmmaker who insisted on doing a walk with me around the perimeter that looked down to Madi Khola River, several hundred metres below. It seems everything in the Himalayas is on a colossal scale, and I found myself keeping well back from the cliff edge. It was made of a gravelly base and looked like it could collapse at any time. My new-found Russian friend took copious photos of me with the mountains behind. I wondered what Russian website I would end up on, and what captions would be added! It was time to go, and I wondered if I should leave my bank details for any future royalty payments. Perhaps Vladimir Putin would be contacting me for a joint 'shirtless' photo shoot on horseback!

The evening was very cold – minus ten degrees according to the guesthouse owner – who most likely did not own a thermometer, but knew how to keep the tourists happy. As I watched the snow falling outside I was reminded that it was in fact Christmas, and I thought of the beautiful family dinners that were happening back home. I wasn't really too soulful; there were other guests, and I had ordered pizza for dinner.

I certainly needed a break from dal baht, the traditional Nepalese dish made from lentils; it was highly nutritious, but once per week was enough for me. The locals ate it with their hands, which I could not do, but I can only speak glowingly of the food I had enjoyed on this trip. The Nepalese are wonderful farmers, and everywhere I went I saw fresh crops of vegetables and orchards of fruit; they had been doing this on the same terraced mountainsides for thousands of years. I had developed a wonderful respect and love for these people.

What's more, the locals had really learnt to cater to the Western pallet with wholesome pizza, pasta, noodles, eggs done almost any way, and their beer is delicious; however, at US$5/500ml bottle up here in the mountains, I was rationed to one per week. It had to be carried in by horseback and I so felt for those animals with their large packs of human produce.

I decided to skip coffee and port around the fireside with the locals and the other guest. In reality there was no fireside, only one local, and a young European woman who wasn't really into conversation. Instead I headed to my room with an additional quilt and snuggled into my sleeping bag to dream of Christmas dinners and family gifts, and the sweltering heat that is my home in Brisbane, Australia. It can be the other extreme of this Himalayan cold, when the humidity reaches ninety-eight percent and the temperature is thirty-five-plus degrees Celcius. Yuk! I was loving being in my sleeping bag and quilt, knowing the snow was falling ever so gently. All was well in my world.

I do have a certain discomfort with Christmas in the West though, mostly due to the over-commercialisation of gifts and more gifts – and more gifts! I love to hear of families who place a $10 limit on gifts or who give more generously to charities such as UNHCR, Australian Wildlife Conservancy, or The Pencil Tree, to name just a few reputable organisations. We are spilling over with 'stuff' in the West and 'stuff' that simply doesn't make us happy.

On a more personal note, since my sister was killed before my eyes in a bushwalking accident on 10 December 1974, Christmas has rarely held that excited wonder and joy of giving for me, particularly when someone so dear was taken from my family's life, even if 44 years on. However, my three children at a very young age certainly brought me great joy at this festive time of year and there was much to celebrate. And on this particular Christmas day, high in the Himalayan Mountains I was truly happy, and I can say that my sister's spirit of adventure was with me.

> **DETERMINATION, WITH AN OPTIMISTIC ATTITUDE, IS THE KEY FACTOR FOR SUCCESS.**

HIS HOLINESS, THE 14TH DALAI LAMA

03

CHAPTER

RED SYMBOLIZES FIRE

BOUND FOR POKHARA

"AND AS WE LET OUR OWN LIGHT SHINE, WE UNCONSCIOUSLY GIVE OTHER PEOPLE PERMISSION TO DO THE SAME. AS WE ARE LIBERATED FROM OUR OWN FEAR, OUR PRESENCE AUTOMATICALLY LIBERATES OTHERS."

Marianne Williamson

Day 17, and I was heading to Pokhara with my skates on. My trip had a new focus – to get to Pokhara with my five hundred rupee (US$50) budget, generously supplied by my two Canadian friends. It was a minimum of four days trekking, and the last section of seven hours would be by jeep. My body was in good shape; fit, toned, and ready to cross country. As beautiful as the Himalayas are, it was time to go and the way I moved reflected that. I could only give thanks to my fifty-six-year-old body that had always carried me so well, and this trip was no exception.

Dear Akash commented several times – when we liked each other – that "you walk like a twenty-year-old"! Now that really was a compliment coming from a young man so skilled in these mountains. He told me he had been a porter before he rose in rank to the esteemed 'guide' position, and now only carried a seven-kilogram pack on this trip – a wallet shoulder strap bristling with rolls of Nepalese rupees and US dollars. Akash was to assist me with changing my US dollars when it was discovered the ATMs in Jomsom would not accept my Visa card, yet in Pokhara that wasn't an issue. It seems that is how things work up here in the rarefied atmosphere. What's more, the locals in these more remote areas don't seem interested in US dollars, which possibly says a lot for the buoyant economy of Nepal.

My biggest mistake was not withdrawing enough rupees before we took off from Pokhara. Around twenty thousand rupees would have been appropriate: however, I didn't know fully how this controlling system of finances worked, especially as I had already paid US$50/day back in Kathmandu with the smooth talking yet very affable young man called Kewal who owned the trekking company. This was an all-in-one package including a very plush bus from Kathmandu, except for all the little extras as I mentioned before!

Kewal must have seen me coming at one hundred metres as I walked through customs at Tribhuvan International Airport,

LEFT: *Pokhara rowing boats on Phewa Tal, second largest lake in Nepal. And the foothills to the Himalaya*

CHAPTER 03

Kathmandu. He had a sharp eye for detail and he knew I would be a very likely candidate for his business. I had all the right gear; back pack, boots and lightweight clothing. When he approached me like some expert game hunter, I was very resistant – especially as I had been in contact with two other guides that friends had connected me with by email from Australia.

It just so happened his office was very near my hotel, the Kathmandu Garden Hotel in Thamel, so I accepted his taxi ride. He talked with me and his assistants almost the whole way to his office. He was a very good salesperson and his English was excellent; what's more, he dressed smartly in a clean light grey suit and came across as a very honest person … which he was. He delivered as he said, and he was within the budget I had determined back home. So this was why I went with him, and I do feel a great warmth and respect for him being the young entrepreneur he was. My respect has not waned on that account; he just needs to train his guides to back off and stand down when requested! I think Akash must have been a Gurkha in a past life, bless his socks! Determined and bloody minded – a bit like me really … crash, bang, clash!

I was aiming for the village of Bamboo, which we had passed on the way up to the base camps. It had a beautiful guesthouse perched on the edge of the valley, with the Modi Khola River flowing at a great rate just one hundred metres below. I enjoyed afternoon tea on the deck as my legs had worked hard that day navigating the relentless up and down of stone staircases that just seemed to never end. I was touched by the craftsmanship of the stone staircase builders who most likely go back many generations. I had a mental strategy in place for the very long sections: I would aim for a spot perhaps one hundred metres up and I would go for it, rest a little, and then do it again and again … and again! It was in these places that I would watch the teams of horses laden with tourist goods coming and going, and I felt for these beautiful animals toiling in another human created industry.

After tea, I could not resist walking around and underneath the teahouse/dining hall to see what the foundations and footings were like. It was an interesting perusal, and I thank the Gods that salt water corrosion was not part of the environmental factors here. The steel placement was visible from the concrete in several places, but then this was Nepal and accomplishing any building project here was cause for remarkable celebration.

The night was cold but the snow had gone, and the weather looked to continue very favourably. In fact, this whole trip had been very favourable in terms of weather, apart from the minus-fifteen degrees and frostbite back at Thorong La Pass. Ahh – what I put my Southeast Queensland fingers through! They have now forgiven me, but I have been given strict instructions by my fingertips to stock up next time with the correct hand-warming gear called Himalayan-grade gloves! Sounds so very simple really, and self-protective.

The following day, I continued heading south-west to Ghandruk, a sizeable village with over thirty-eight hotels and a micro-hydroelectric plant which was developed in the 1980s to cope with growing electricity demands brought on mostly by tourism. It requires no dam – just a simple turbine mounted on the side of the valley and a two-hundred-millimetre water pipe feeding it. The process is simple and effective, and helps to preserve the natural timber resources – and their reliance on kerosene, which has to be brought in by pack horse. Ghandruk is a remote village that attracts tens of thousands of guests per year; its elevation and natural mountain beauty are stunning. (15)

I wanted to push on to Kimche, a small village with road access to Pokhara, where I could connect with a jeep the following day. It was another three hour walk through some absolutely beautiful oak forest, bamboo, rhododendrons, and deep valleys where the Modi Khola River continued to flow. Throughout my Himalayan trek I was impressed by the local engineering of bridges that most likely spanned back countless generations. In a country so full of rivers – and usually very large rivers – there needs to be a way of crossing them safely.

Bazam bridges are used – a traditional method of bridge-building which jeeps can cross – and they use 200x200mm sections of timber or larger depending on the bridge span; they criss-crossed them backwards and forwards with the aim to bridge the span of the river. They are self-supporting and a very clever method of engineering. I took photos of some very precarious structures that were used for foot traffic and livestock, which looked like they could be washed away during the next wet season.

In recent years, the 40mm steel wire construction method is used more and more especially for the tourist crossings, many of which span fifty metres or more. They are well-built and very stable.

It turns out that a Swiss organisation called Helvetas has been doing these projects since 2009 and have since built over 4,000 trail bridges in the Himalayas and other regions of Nepal. I was fairly sure I had walked over fifty such bridges on the Annapurna Circuit and Base Camp, some spanning twenty metres, with others more than fifty. They all had the standard forty-millimetre cable in binds of one, two, or three, with a base plate made of a galvanised section which became the walking platform. It was brilliant in design and in construction; simple to implement in almost any river crossing, and would last for many years, river levels permitting. (16)

Very near Ghandruk was a small village called Kyumi, situated on the very high banks of the mighty Modi Khola River, and to get to it I had to weave my way down off the main Ghandruk track and back up the other side. This would get me to Kimche, where I would spend the night and meet the jeep that would take me to Pokhara – Day 21, and the conclusion of my Himalayan adventure!

There were teams of horses loaded with gravel, and signs everywhere to look out for "Bridge Works". I could hear the sound of jack hammers, and as I rounded the corner into the village there it was on both sides of this massive river crossing; perhaps five hundred metres apart, teams of men and most likely women were digging footings for this bigger than big bridge-build. I have never seen such a large suspension bridge before. The gravel on my side of the river was being taken away by the teams of horses and on the eastern side heading to Landruk – another tourist Mecca – the workers were just pushing the gravel over the edge into the river. It was like a massive scar that no doubt would heal in a year or two once the work was complete.

I assumed this would be another Helvetas engineering masterpiece; they seemed to have no boundaries in their efforts to help the Nepalese people as well as the buoyant tourist industry that sustains them well. The river, some hundred or more metres below, was never going to reach this monster of all bridges. A low flying aircraft or helicopter would be the only threat to its demise and that was very, very unlikely. Go the Swiss, I say!

I reached Kimche in the late afternoon. It had been a long day of walking at a strong pace and the fact is that I got 'misplaced'

... which is different from being 'lost'! I never use that word even in the thickest of the World Heritage Rainforest back in my home territory of Lamington National Park – just 'misplaced', thank you! It took me about an hour and a half to work it out ... where was the bloody guide when I needed him! Hah! The pleasure of being on my own, walking on my own, making every decision for myself, and talking to lovely foreign guests by myself was delightful! It was worth every moment of my one-and-a-half-hour 'misplacement'. So there!

PREVIOUS PAGE: *Foothills of the Himalayas from Dovan*
ABOVE: *Carrying excavation material from the new bridge*
MIDDLE: *Porters carrying roof sheeting*
RIGHT: *Carpenter's plane, Dovan*

Kimche was a delightful tourist town bolted onto a very steep landscape, no real surprise seeing I was in the Himalayas. I found a hotel close to the car park where the jeep would come at nine o'clock in the morning; I simply had to get on that jeep, as my budget was almost spent. In fact I estimated I would get back to Pokhara with about eighty rupees – less than US$1 – in my wallet. It is only recently that jeeps have come this far up. In the past, tourists had to go to Nayapul, which was another day's hike, to meet the bus. Under the circumstances I really just wanted to get to Pokhara, draw out copious quantities of rupees, half drown in Gurkha beer, have a haircut and many tasty meals, walk around the many trekking shops, have a massage, wash my clothes and watch them dry in the winter sun, drink more Gurkha beer, buy gifts for family and friends and stay in my favourite accommodation, the Hotel Yeti. These were the things I dreamt of, and I was just an eight-hour jeep drive away so long as the driver kept a firm grip on the road.

My night in Kimche, at 1,640 metres, was very relaxing and I talked with a young Scottish couple who were just setting off with their guide, but only for seven days. I told them my story and they listened with interest. There was another large group of Indian tourists who I saw in many places. One Indian man was very warm and welcoming to me as he had been working in Perth installing some new software package for the Perth Hospital. He couldn't say enough good things about the Australian staff of this hospital, and more generally about Aussies and our good spirit. I felt very proud and humble that such good will was being carried across the globe by my fellow Australians.

I was in bed by 8.00pm, exhausted by my twenty-one-day achievement, but there was a lot more exhaustion to come when I got back to Australia and the thirty-eight-degree heat and humidity that had enveloped Brisbane and much of Australia.

I was up early and met my young Dutch friends at the jeep station; we had crossed paths for the last week or so, and it was delightful to share a long jeep ride to Pokhara with them. Watching them together was like seeing two lovebirds chirping and cooing and smooching away. Perhaps it was the high altitude, but they certainly showed me that true love was alive and thriving.

The rest of the jeep was filled with Nepalese people – twelve passengers in total. I was jammed in the back with another man and two women eating packs of dry noodles. We had two empty 12kg gas bottles under our feet just to add to the general feeling of being in an over-crowded developing nation. But I sighed with relief when I thought about the treasures I would enjoy in Pokhara.

The trip was nearly eight hours over mostly reasonable – mostly dirt – roads, and there were many stops along the way to drop things off and pick up other cargo. And so it went all the way to Pokhara, with lots of Nepalese music and chatter. These were the things I recorded to make into one-hour eclectic sound stories for radio. I am currently working on these, and they will form part of the Men's and Women's Stories on SoundCloud.

From where our friendly jeep driver dropped us, I walked down to the main street and found the very lovely Hotel Yeti, right next to the action of the New Year celebrations, which run for five days in Pokhara and started the very night I arrived. It was the twenty-eighth of December 2017, and the conclusion of my twenty-one days in the Himalayas. Twenty-one days in the Himalayas; it just sounds so lovely ... and it was!

The room was beautiful, and at US$15/night one would expect it to be. My host was delightful and she told me the story of how she and her husband renovated this hotel after her grandparents had left it to her ten years ago. They had done a very professional job with the help of many very capable Nepalese tradespeople I would think.

My first priority was a hot shower, some fresh clothes, and the washing of my dirty clothes which I hung all around the room, very tastefully I thought. A visit to the ATM across the street was the next priority. This was a tourist Mecca with more than ten ATMs available. The way it worked was to keep rotating in the secure room till you found one that worked; it took me three goes – a western woman was having much worse luck - it's like the gods have some influence here on who will get their money; similar to 'who will climb the mountain' – the gods will decide!

ABOVE: *Steel gate to private residence in Pokhara*
MIDDLE: *New Year's festivities in Pokhara*
RIGHT: *Men at work – just like home except for steel capped boots and helmet*

I withdrew a cool 12,000 rupees (US$120); now that is comfort money in these parts. I went back to the hotel restaurant for a delightful meal of dal baht and chicken and two 500ml bottles of Gurkha beer – a celebration, even if alone, of my twenty-one days in the Himalayas. The passing street parade and on-going preparations for the evening were wonderful to watch, and my friendly host came and went as she worked the floor and her customers. It was truly lovely to be here. I later met her husband who was an equally charming young man. It turns out they had both worked and lived in Melbourne for several years; their English was excellent, and I wished them all the best Aussie luck.

My next priority was to head back around the corner to the barber I had spotted on my arrival. He was a gentleman in his forties and highly skilled with his cutters and scissors. It was set up like a Western barbershop, with a large mirror and chair that swivelled and went up and down. I just felt so relaxed and happy with my achievement and my new-found love for the Nepalese people. I vowed to come again and not just trek but help in any way I could with a charity that a friend had set up some five years before to help Tibetan and Nepalese children: The Pencil Tree Charity.

With the haircut finished I was offered a back and shoulder massage as I sat in the chair. As it turned out he offered just about any type of massage imaginable right there in his chair, and in full view of the world. As relaxed and comfortable as I was, my budget was spent at this particular venue. I had after all come for a haircut. I was concerned if I didn't say no, God only knew where he was heading. I paid the man his very specific tourist price – the same as that of home, which left me feeling quite possibly ripped off – but I was on too much of a high to argue. Besides, it was nearly New Year's Eve. Off I went, back down to the growing hordes on the main lakeside street as the sun was setting.

ABOVE: *A Dad with his baby girl – they were selling every type of legume known to Nepal*

MIDDLE: *Gurkha Museum – a visit for my Father, Pokhura*

RIGHT: *Big banana shopping with Akash en route to Besisahar*

People come from miles around for this celebration, and Indians seemed to be the main foreign guests; there were a smattering of Westerners and the party was building. I began to think that Pokhara had more bars and hotels than Las Vegas – not to mention the dance halls. I didn't really feel like going on my own, so I headed down to where the trekking shops were. I wanted a few clothing goods that are copies made in Nepal, but generally of reasonable quality. Long pants, a jacket, socks, and a shirt were all I needed and they were less than half the price of home. I did not discover till I got back to Kathmandu that the North Face day pack that I bought on arrival in Thamel was a very poor copy that needed much tender adjustment to be workable – I gave it to Lifeline when I got home. I am sure the genuine North Face company would have sold me a wonderful day pack for double what I paid for this junky copy, and I would have been a happy customer. My mistake!

MY ARRIVAL IN POKHARA

I had met Akash in Pokhara on the eighth day of December after arriving by luxury coach from Kathmandu – and I mean an extraordinary luxury coach with plush vinyl seats only three across. They were wide enough for any size bottom. Kewal only wanted the best for his clients, and the eight-hour drive stopped at a five-star hotel for lunch. We passed several of the local buses which were crowded, dirty and in some cases downright dangerous.

Only a few weeks before I arrived, there had been a horrendous accident in which most of the passengers onboard were killed as the bus crashed through a guard rail and plunged down a hundred metres or more into the icy waters below. God knows what bedlam must have ensured onboard. I also saw the remains of other busses on the side of the road that looked to have been in horrendous head-on collisions. It was best not to watch the skills and manoeuvring of the bus driver and just hope we would arrive at our destination in one piece.

Before leaving Pokhara on Day 1, Akash and I visited the Gurkha Memorial Museum on the outskirts of town, well away from the tourist noise. It was a very proud two-storey building which I visited out of respect for my own father, who served in the British Army at the tail end of World War II. The Gurkhas are a fearsome and elite fighting force of Nepal that gained recognition by the British in the early 1800s, when Nepal was a colony of Great Britain, and to this day they still serve as part of the British Army.

The Gurkha regiments have served on many fronts since their inception in 1815 – the most notable being the Gallipoli campaign of 1915; they were the first regiment to arrive and the last to leave. In World War I more than 200,000 Gurkhas served, and there were over 20,000 casualties. Nearly 2,000 gallantry awards were given for their service. In World War II there were ten Gurkha regiments deployed, and from 1858 to 1965 the Gurkhas had won twenty-six Victoria Crosses. In 2007, women were allowed to join this formidable fighting force. [17]

RIGHT: *Besisahar at dawn – they grow vegetables anywhere*

The museum was filled with hundreds of photos chronicling the Gurkha regiments' development, training, and missions since their inception. I felt my father walking with me as I wandered among the display cabinets of uniforms and other military paraphernalia. He was very proud of their commitment and loyalty to the British Army. Each year there are up to seventeen thousand applications for the Gurkha regiments, but only two hundred and thirty are accepted; the process and training to become enlisted is thorough. (18)

In many of the villages around the Annapurna Circuit I came across water taps that had been installed by the Gurkhas. They had used their characteristic regiment emblem which is two knives called Khukuri, crossed over – and placed that emblem on each of the timber tap mounts. These knives are about three hundred millimetres long with a blade that curves forward and form the Gurkha emblem and since the regiment's inception of 1815, it remains their emblem to this day.

Akash and I caught a local bus to Besisahar, a six-hour journey through the foothills of the Himalayas. It was mostly farming country with very prosperous towns featuring three-storey houses that looked very grand. I wondered how they were financed. We stayed the night in Besisahar, at a friendly hotel with a rooftop garden where I recorded roosters crowing before dawn. They woke me up, so I thought I would head up to the roof to record the sounds of this sizeable town – one of the epicentres of the Himalayas in terms of goods and merchandise supply.

After dinner the previous night, I had walked out into a small forecourt to see three women – one holding a very new baby – and a small fire was burning where they were warming oil to rub into the little baby's skin. It was very moving to see such tenderness. I assumed dad was the man preparing food and now washing up, and they were very happy for me to stand there and take photos. It was a deeply moving scene, and I presume the warm oil was some rather beautiful welcoming into the world. I felt honoured to be allowed to witness the process. I remembered how the birth of my three children brought so much loving attention from family and friends, especially the grandmas who seem to just understand the human cycle at a very deep level.

Our jeep was to leave at 8:00am and we walked up the street to where it departed. It looked like ten people were already inside,

LEFT: *The prettiest police I've ever seen, Besisahar*

and we would make twelve. As I waited for last minute goods to be piled on top, I bumped into two very beautiful young policewomen, each dressed in blue jumpers with long blue pants, black boots, and carrying a 1.2m timber staff. They were just way too pretty to be police – no offence intended. They very kindly agreed to a photo and giggled to themselves at this silly tourist. They must have thought I was rather humorous as I headed off to explore the high country and left them to attend to important police duties! How I dreamt of being a villain in their town and being arrested by them in all sorts of forcible ways ... handcuffs, being jumped on and made to submit to their beauty. Ahh! It would have been delightful – I mean terrible – a most amusing fantasy at least – just get in the Jeep and go!

The option to drive to Chame by Jeep was a pre-determined Kewal choice – it's otherwise a three day walk which follows a dirt road in many places, so it seemed like a good option. It was an eight-hour drive that, at times, left me looking in the opposite direction as the roaring Marsyangdi Nadi River was more than one hundred metres below. God knows why they built this road, but the answer is obvious, I suppose – to save the horses that once carried the goods for tourists. Or perhaps the horses can no longer keep up with the estimated sixty thousand tourists that come to the Annapurna every year.

It was a very interesting drive that took us through farming country, timber sawmills, and the obligatory tourist villages that were fortunately closed for the winter. I had my little digital recorder going for at least two hours of the time we were driving. The men were talking away to each other, and the music was playing. It was all too good to be true as I was embarking on my Himalayan expedition and the mountains were getting bigger by the hour.

One of the men and his assistant were biologists working for a university in Kathmandu, and they had come out here to monitor the numbers of blue sheep and snow leopards. There would be several times that Akash and I would see the blue sheep that usually live above 3,000 metres, as does the snow leopard, though in less populated areas.

In total we saw about fifty blue sheep – or bharal as they are called locally. They seemed to be doing well in groups of up to a dozen, and on first appearance they looked more like goats.

They are given that name because they have a blue tinge to their otherwise grey coat and white underbelly. The males have an impressive set of curled horns that can be nearly a metre across; hence the need to protect them, as they have been hunted almost to extinction since the late 1800s. Today their numbers have increased to the point that they are low on the endangered species list, thanks to the work of this Nepalese biologist from the university in Kathmandu.

We didn't see the snow leopard – or ounce as it is known locally – anywhere, but that doesn't mean they didn't see us. They are very quiet and expert hunters. It is estimated that between four and nine thousand snow leopards are still in the wild in various parts of the world. In the Himalayas it is estimated three to five hundred still roam wild. They are most beautiful to look at with their characteristic spotted coat, extra-large paws for snow travel, and a large bushy tail to help with balancing their big frame – similar in size to that of a large dog. (19)

ABOVE: *Marsyangdi Nadi river and Tal township built on an alluvial plain*
MIDDLE: *Our overloaded jeep and flat tyre, just an hours walk to Chame*
RIGHT: *These women do this every autumn to provide warmth for their animals throughout winter*

I saw a shocking photo from the late 1800s in the government office in Chomrong of an estimated fifty or more snow leopard skins lying stretched across timber frames drying in the sun; two 'proud Europeans' were holding their rifles, standing with a few of the natives in the background. Thank God, we have grown in knowledge and intelligence since that time! Such destructive, male machismo nonsense; perhaps taking one or even two could be justified in those times, but not fifty or more!

The yak is another Himalayan gem. I thought we saw about fifty of them with their own colourful neck bells, but I was later told that what we actually saw were hybrid cows with many of the yak's characteristics but not pure bred wild yak, which are distinguished by their long fur that skirts past their knees. There is also the characteristic fatty tail – up to 300mm wide and 600mm long – with so much hair that it is used to swat flies, among more sacred uses. Another distinctive characteristic is its large head, which I saw screwed to many hotel entrances – perhaps that is the reason the purebreds are in such short supply.

I discovered through a little research that what I had seen was a descendent of the wild yak which was, in fact, on the endangered list with an estimate of only one hundred and seventy remaining; they are believed to be scattered across Northern Tibet and parts of China. They are the largest of the bovids which have a conical hoof and include goats, cows, kudu, and wildebeests. They are generally found at around 3,500 metres elevation and are now extinct in Nepal and Bhutan. They are also fair game for the snow leopard. [20]

The very large cattle we did see, that were of a similar genetic make-up to yaks, were valuable animals, providing butter, cheese, meat, skin, as well as head decorations on many of the hotels as we passed; a little like "my horn is bigger than your horn". I'm very sure the poor bovids would prefer the open pastures to that rather male human condition of showing off ones' horn. Interestingly enough, they don't make good pack animals as their backs do not tolerate excessive weight. Their wool, however, makes the most delightful scarves, gloves, socks and many more very useful things to keep warm in the Himalayas. A pair of yak gloves over Thorong La Pass would have been very handy in avoiding months of pain, numbing discomfort, and layers and layers of dead skin.

I had the good fortune to try yak meat and yes, it is delicious, and especially so in the cold mountain air. They are considered sacred and most certainly revered by the people of the Himalayas for the countless sacrifices the animal makes for these people. How many of us in the West give thanks to our humble yet wonderful cows that give so much to us. I am not a big meat eater and really cannot remember the last Aussie barbeque I hosted and my quest is to continue eating much less meat. The need for lower impact food sources across the planet grows every day, with global warming quite clearly in our sights.

The hotel in Chame was most delightful, with a warm and cosy dining hall, and lots of maps and photos on the walls, in particular a huge map of Tibet with a large photo of Lhasa and the Potala Palace, which was built on the mountainside in the early 1700s. This was where the 14th Dalai Lama used to live before the Chinese decided he would be safer in Northern India, or anywhere but his place of birth, Tibet. How dare the Dalai Lama think Tibet is his home just because he was born there with such a very long lineage? The reality of this rather sad joke is nothing more than Chinese expansionism, and after my trip to the Himalayas and seeing firsthand where Chinese 'investment' is going in the Annapurna region alone, it only reinforces to me that their main purpose and goal is harnessing water and exploiting many rich mining opportunities. In short: expansionism!

ABOVE: *The friendly staff at our Chame hotel*
MIDDLE: *Traditional bridge called a Bazam*
RIGHT: *Akash leaving the very new Nepal Manang Tibetan Buddhist Temple*

The Tibetan Plateau has an estimated mining value of US$128 billion. It is twice the size of Texas – almost 1.5million m2 – and as my research showed, it is further estimated that it contains a billion tonnes of rich iron ore, forty million tonnes of copper, and over forty million tonnes of lead and zinc – just the sort of materials needed for the burgeoning dragon economy of China. It's a shame the Tibetan waters can't put that particular flaming fire out. Let's not forget the threatened species including the snow leopard, wild yak, and rare antelope that truly will not survive with these massive mining projects operating.

In many ways this mining enterprise had begun when the rail line to Tibet was completed in 2006; but that, of course, is supposed to carry Tibetan tourists down to Beijing for some much-needed R and R. I heard just yesterday the Dalai Lama was buying his first ticket for his next holiday to Tibet – not bloody likely! (21)

I find it is infuriating to read of Chinese activities around these developments and the mining projects which will, in their opinion, benefit the natural environment by providing roads to the area.

The people who have lived in that region for thousands of years will also be able to use those roads to relocate to the motherland of China, or even Lhasa if they must – somehow, I doubt those people will want to move if not for China's 'big stick' in the shape of an enormous and smelly industrialised dragon. (22)

"China has now moved millions of Tibetan nomads from their traditional grasslands to urban settlements, opening their land for the extraction of resources and ending traditional agricultural practices which have sustained and protected the Tibetan environment for centuries." (23)

ABOVE: *Little boy in his home in the Himalayas*
MIDDLE: *The prayer wheels at Chame*
RIGHT: *My guide Akash, standing next to just one of his 'surprises for the day'*
NEXT PAGE: *Chinese owned Sinohydro-Sagarmatha Power Company plant, just north of Syange*

I am sure the thousands of Tibetan refugees living in Nepal and Northern India would much prefer this relocation rather than remaining in what has been their homeland and tradition for thousands of years. I'm melting under the table here as I try to make light about one of the world's great travesties – China's invasion of Tibet, which started in 1959 and continues to this day – with the Fourteenth Dalai Lama, the true leader of Tibet, having to live in exile in fear of his life. We in the West don't give a toss because of our governments' trade deals with China, from which we are all benefitting. It's just wrong! (24)

In a much smaller room to the side of the dining room – back in our lovely hotel in Chame – there was a central steel fire drum, about the size of a forty-four-gallon drum, fuelled by timber most likely collected from the local sawmills. There were perhaps twenty seats set in an oval shape around this big grey drum. No doubt many hiking stories were told here, but that night there were only five guests ... just the way I liked it.

> "WHEN YOU PEOPLE CAME TO OUR LAND IT WAS NOT WITH OPEN ARMS BUT WITH BIBLES AND GUNS AND DISEASE. YOU TOOK OUR LAND. YOU KILLED US WITH YOUR GUNS AND DISEASE, THEN HAD THE ARROGANCE TO CALL US GODLESS SAVAGES."

NORTH AMERICAN INDIAN

04
CHAPTER

GREEN SYMBOLIZES WATER

TILICHO TAL LAKE, 4,920 METRES ABOVE SEA LEVEL

"LOVE AND COMPASSION ARE NECESSITIES, NOT LUXURIES. WITHOUT THEM HUMANITY CANNOT SURVIVE"
Dalai Lama

On Day 2 our walk took us through the prosperous and industrious village of Chame; I noted a small hydro-electricity plant operating on one of the fast-flowing streams that moved through the town. Ingenious, I thought, and not much bigger than the drum we sat around the night before, with four hand-sized fins that whirred at the speed of the water.

Akash said he had a cultural sight in store for me and sure enough, halfway through the village, we came to a Buddhist prayer wheel almost three metres high and two metres in diameter, turning inside a small building beautifully decorated with the Buddhist colours of red, blue, green, and gold. There were also prayer flags that ran across the track and back again; they danced in the breeze of a beautifully fresh December morning, with the mountain presence felt but not quite visible just yet. It would be today that I would first view Annapurna III, at 7,555 metres the largest mountain I have ever seen so close. I was already falling in love with Nepal and its resilient, friendly people.

It is the local custom to pull these large prayer wheels in a clockwise direction by holding the handle that spans the circumference while at the same time reciting the six ohms: Om Mani Padme Hum, or any other of the two million prayers the Buddhists have. Enlightenment is always the aim of this gentle guidance, a practice well-honed for over 1,500 years. During their manufacture, the prayer wheels are filled with Buddhist prayers written on paper, rolled, and packed in to give the wheels weight. (25)

According to my source, 'Om' refers to generosity, and purifies pride and ego. It has the Samsaric realm of Deva, which essentially refers to a god-like being with the colour of white. The symbol of the deity is wisdom in the perfect realm of Potala.

LEFT: *The author at Tilicho Tal, the highest lake for its size on the planet, 4,920 metres*

'Ma' refers to ethics, and purifies lust for entertainment. It has the Samsaric realm of Asuras, which refers to a minor deity with the colour of green. The symbol of the deity is compassion to be born in the perfect realm of Potala.

'Ni' refers to patience, and purifies passion and desire. It has the Samsaric realm of Humans with the colour of yellow. The symbol of the deity is body, speech, mind quality, and activity to be born into a feminine form.

'Pad' refers to diligence, and purifies ignorance and prejudice. It has the Samsaric realm of Animals with the colour blue. The symbol of the deity is equanimity and to be born into the protector, Chenrezig, the compassion of all Buddhas.

'Me' refers to renunciation, and purifies greed and possessiveness. It has the Samsaric realm of Pretas [26] or hungry ghosts with the colour of red. The symbol of the deity is bliss and to be born into the perfect realm of Potala.

And finally, 'Hum' refers to wisdom, and purifies aggression and hatred. It has the Samsaric realm of Naraka – or purgatory or hell – with the colour of black. The symbol of the deity is quality of compassion; to be born in the presence of the Lotus Throne of Chenrezig. [27]

On the edge of town, as with every Himalayan village, there was a long set of prayer wheels. The area was fifty metres or more in length, containing around one hundred prayer wheels made of a pressed metal brass with the 'Om', 'Mani', 'Padme' and 'Hum' pressed into the metal. Individually they measured about four hundred millimetres high and two hundred and fifty millimetres in diameter. Some are left in their natural brass colour and others are painted, and over time the colours wear with all the hands that seek the 'meritorious effect' from the process of turning the wheel of Dharma, or cosmic law and order. [28]

Akash took me to the hot springs just on the edge of town; we didn't slide into the hot waters for some reason – perhaps because, at Day 2, our legs were fresh – but the waters certainly were hot and smelled of the rich mineral content which is so healing for aching muscles. The water flowed from five steel pipes dug into the mountainside, fifty millimetres in diameter, with steam rising off them. The water plunged into a pool half a metre deep, and this helped to cool everything down. They then overflowed into the raging Marsyangdi Nadi River below. A concrete pool approximately five metres square had been built with a set of stairs to climb in and out of the healing waters.

The walk that day was extraordinary, and I was beginning to feel part of the Himalayas. The surrounding mountains were well over 6,000 metres and offered consistent views to the south-west of Annapurna II at 7,937 metres, Annapurna IV at 7,525 metres, and Annapurna III at 7,555 metres. We also walked around the famous Swargadwari Danda, which is a massive rock formation that curves around to the north and south for five kilometres, with an elevation of over 1,500 metres. The trail at this point, which passed through conifer forests, was at over 3,000 metres. It was time to start preparing for the high altitude and our crossing of Thorong La Pass at 5,416 metres in just five days time.

ABOVE: *A Yak skin bed*
MIDDLE: *Looking south-east to the Upper Pisang*
RIGHT: *One of the many Yak heads above the hotel entrances*

I had brought Diamox with me and started taking it; 250mg morning and night when we reached the very beautiful town of Manang, at 3,540 metres. It helps to prevent, though certainly not cure, altitude sickness. Akash was always reminding me to eat the local garlic soup, which was very tasty – but once a day was my limit. The best acclimatization tool is time. We spent two nights in Manang, which swells in size to several thousand when the tourists come in their droves in the main tourist months of April and October. With it being December and quite cold, the tourists had mostly all gone; our rather lovely hotel had perhaps fifty guests; perfect! I was on the second level with a view across the river flats, which must have been a kilometre wide at this point. It wound its way down the valley with the Annapurnas to the south-west, and other mountains rising over 6,000 metres to the north-east.

At Upper Pisang we headed north to climb to the view-point that looked north-west to Manang, and south-east to the extraordinary curving wall of Swargadwari Danda, with dustings of snow on one section to the north where it was at its highest, 4,895 metres. This steady climb took three hours, and was an elevation gain of almost 1,500 metres. I think this was Akash's way of gauging how I would go on the main pass both in terms of fitness and the high elevations he took us to. You will be pleased to know he gave me a green light – my body, mind, and soul loved being here. It was my time, in so many ways! The Himalayas were just a very good extension of that.

LEFT: *Marsyangdi Nadi river*
ABOVE: *Healthy, happy child with her mum in Nyawal*
MIDDLE: *Looking south-west towards Annapurna III*
RIGHT: *Marsyangdi Nadi river with a Bazam bridge in the foreground*

Before we reached Manang there was a small village called Braka; what made this village so special was the Buddhist monastery that rose up the mountainside. It was somewhat similar to Potala Palace in Lhasa, but half the size. We planned to visit the next day, which was to be our rest day in Manang, but most importantly our first acclimatisation day.

We arrived in Manang mid-afternoon and went to a beautiful hotel with the mandatory yak head hanging off the frontage, and another yak head air-drying on a balcony near my room. The yak was revered for its strength and general goodness; perhaps sacred is a more apt description, although it would have been enjoyable to see a whole one walking around town with its body, legs, and tail naturally attached. Somewhere on this leg – no pun intended – I had seen the skin of a yak spread out on a deck with a family laying on it in the winter sun; but where were the other bits of the yak that made them whole?

Akash was eager to show me the latest in Buddhist temples built right there in Manang, and only finished in 2017. It was less than

an hour's climb, positioned on the edge of town to the north-east. The view up and down the valley was extraordinary enough, but the building with the intricate wood work around the door was mesmerizing, to say the least. They had carved ten-millimetre squares built up in stacks of perhaps ten high, and this pattern followed in two directions all the way around the door. I wondered if they had been cut with a jigsaw or router back at 'Buddhist Builders, Inc' in Kathmandu, as they were just too perfect to be hand-carved.

The whole structure was eight square metres, but knowing the Buddhists there would be an exact size to represent the spiritual component of the universe mixed in with enough deities to fill every metre from sea level to where we currently were at 3,450 metres plus a bit! The Nepalese people know how to appreciate and worship their life, and it's really not about personal wealth. It is much more a collective wealth, and this is perhaps something we in the West need to hear ... loudly!

LEFT: *Prayer wheel wall, Upper Pisang*
ABOVE: *Juniper smoke purifying the world*
MIDDLE: *Prayer wheel in Upper Pisang*
RIGHT: *Marsyangdi Nadi river*

Dear Akash, at the height of our squabbles some ten days later, would say to me as he walked away in utter frustration: "What is it with you people and money?" But then I wasn't an open wallet to a guiding industry – I really did like him though, very much in fact.

It was almost sunset and I sent Akash on his way back to the hotel to do what guides do at this time of day when they are out in the mountains: sip chai or lemon ginger tea with their guide mates. The raucous squawks of fun and joy from the kitchen were fun to listen to, with a dozen or more hotel staff and guides all sipping their tea. At the hotel just before Lake Tilicho a few of the tourists, including myself, rebelled at this kitchen gathering, as the outside temperature was very much below zero and we wanted the fire lit, but more on this little incident later.

I continued to admire this beautiful Buddhist temple in Manang with its deep red-coloured double doors, and brass door handles the size of small dinner plates. The roof was gold in colour with the most intricate dragon heads on each of the twelve structural hips, which were also gold in colour. They were carved in wood, approximately six hundred millimetres long, and mounted on the end of the timber hips so that they stood about three hundred millimetres high. The rafters were the same dark red colour as the front doors, with blue soffits to match the sky and heavens above.

As I walked inside there was an altar with a gold Buddha one metre high and adorned with brass relief figurines and so much other decoration that it is almost too much to describe. Just past the entrance, as I headed to the altar, there was a raised ceiling to at least five metres. Once again, the timber design was intricate and stepped up another metre, with the use of different colours of blue, red, yellow, green – and many shades thereof.

ABOVE: *Yak cheese for sale in Manang*
MIDDLE: *Bakery delights in Manang*
RIGHT: *Sanskrit on the prayer wall at Braka*
FAR RIGHT: *A newly renovated Tibetan Buddhist Gompa near Braka with Annapurna III and I in the background*

Outside, not far from the entrance, was a two metre by one metre tray of juniper leaves drying in the last of the wintery sunlight. It is a sacred Buddhist incense that they burn and smoke to purify and uplift spirit and mind; I saw it being smoked in many homes, usually just outside the doorway. At this temple, in the far corner of the grounds that overlooked the village of Manang, was a stone vessel about one and half metres long by six hundred millimetres wide and four hundred millimetres deep; they would fill it with juniper leaves and smoke and purify the whole village in one daily burning – how's that for a healthy community service? It smelled earthy and holier than ... you can fill in the blank!

Nightfall was approaching so I began my descent to the hotel, which was quite busy with perhaps fifty guests. In the height of

summer this town would swell to several thousand. The hotel was a beautiful two-storey wooden structure, and every time I went to my room I would walk out onto the balcony - without any railings - and look up and down the mighty river system of Marsyangdi Nadi and out into the mists surrounding Annapurna III, rising in the distance to 7,555 metres. I felt very at home in the Himalayas.

I spent the evening chatting to some of the tourists; a New Zealand group, the same Korean family that we kept passing up and down the valley, and an American woman in her early sixties travelling with a guide. There was a Northern European father and son team who seemed to be tolerating each other, but only just. The Wi-Fi in this tourist village was very good and I was able to connect with a friend at home via messenger on Facebook. The clarity was excellent despite our relative remoteness and 3,540 metre elevation. Ah Facebook, how wonderful!

ABOVE: *Juniper drying in the winter sun, Manang*
MIDDLE: *Door frame design to the Nepal Manang Tibetan Buddhist Temple*
RIGHT: *Firewood collectors at the end of their day, Manang*

Away from the steel drum and fire it was cold, and so when I headed to my room there was little to do but snuggle into the very warm and clean quilts provided. I filled my water bladder and bottles, and treated them with chlorine tablets before getting ready for bed. By the morning the water pipes had frozen – there was no water!

Day 5 was for rest and acclimatisation, so I headed off to visit Gangapurna Tal Lake, just a few hours walk north-west of the village. It meant crossing the Marsyangdi Nadi River by one of the traditional bridges, and climbing a sharp ridge of glacial gravel before climbing further up to a summer teahouse that was closed on this particular icy winter morning. The view back to the village with the roaring river in the foreground was wonderful, with a distinct line between the new tourist town and the older rock wall buildings that were several hundred years old based on its construction.

Before crossing the river, I watched some young boys tobogganing down an icy slide some fifty metres long on a cut-out plastic twenty-litre drum. They were having the time of their lives, and barely noticed me trying my best to photograph the joy on their faces.

In the afternoon Akash was keen to join me and head back down to Braka and the very old monastery, over 500 years old according to him. At the base there was another eight-metre square Buddhist temple, currently under construction, with the same precision to its corners and intricacy of design.

We walked around to the main gate on the west side and began our ascent, passing the very old stone walls of the monastery that

ABOVE: *Boys ice skating near Manang*
MIDDLE: *The blue sheep (or Bharal) skull*
RIGHT: *Little boy at Braka Monastery, south-east of Manang*

most likely served as accommodation to the visiting monks. Much higher up to the east we could see new construction, and above that the most remarkable polished brass Buddha shone in the afternoon sun. It stood almost two metres tall and was perhaps two metres at the base. It was facing south-east to Annapurna II, III and IV; sitting on a white plinth with a curved backing which was also radiant white in colour and which served to lift the remarkable polished metal finish. To describe the detail would be almost foolhardy, as the intricacies that adorned this beautiful piece of art were nothing short of remarkable as he/she looked out across the valley and the Annapurna Mountains. It's always 'he' when it comes to a Buddha according to Akash; however, he/she had some very distinct feminine parts like her waist, breasts, eyebrow liner and red lipstick, not to mention the red and green

stones embedded in her headpiece. I must have spent an hour at this sculpture. It was a work of art – remarkable and indeed created by the Buddhist Gods!

We were unable to enter the main building of the monastery, where there were supposedly many very old statues and fearsome guards for the protection of the Buddhas, as we needed a key and Akash seemed uninterested in finding one, and so we began our descent and return to Manang. It was 'guide time' again with his mates in the kitchen. One can't blame him; I was probably tour number eight for 2017 and he must have missed his family, being away so much.

LEFT: *The golden Buddha, Braka Monastery, fresh out of its wrapping paper*
ABOVE: *Braka resident*
MIDDLE: *Two young French-Canadian men with their musical instruments, Braka Monastery*
RIGHT: *Descending Braka Monastery*

As we descended, the three-metre high vertical prayer flags waved in the breeze with their Buddhist colours flying and combined with hundreds of smaller prayer flags that were strung between the buildings. The flags represent the prayers that are the essence of Tibetan Buddhism, and there are five elements each represented by a colour: blue refers to the sky and space, white represents air and wind, red refers to fire, green refers to water, and yellow represents the earth. All are covered with Buddhist prayers written in Sanskrit, the philosophical language of Buddhism along with several other of the great religions of the world. (29)

It is believed in Tibetan medicine that health and harmony are produced through a balance of these five elements, hence the nature of the Buddhist people here and the spreading of the prayers written on these flags, which are designed to gradually fall apart, spreading their message of health and harmony wherever they fall. I think we could do with a few million of those flags in our Western culture, where money seems to be our focus and where we are willing to mine coal and uranium, and log old-growth forests for the sake of economic growth; never mind building the foundations of our culture like a formal rite of passage for our young men and women to grow through over a lifetime. Traditional peoples practised these skills for thousands of years knowing it was their lineage of survival ... and bugger the coal mine and the list of other destructive practices we Westerners mindlessly pursue.

I believe we have much to learn from the traditional cultures of this planet, where life is not just considered sacred, but it is shown to be so for the next generations. The culture's survival depends on it until, of course, Western culture or some Eastern cultures come along in the name of progress and prosperity with the power to decimate the land like adolescent vandals, not knowing any better than to conquer and exploit.

It seems in 2018 that scenario is happening on the Annapurna, with a huge Eastern power to the north-east already building significant infrastructure in the form of roads and airports, just waiting for when the time is right to include the southern regions of the Himalayas....it could be called Nepal, the south-western province of China. Has a nasty taste to it though – one of expansionism!

What is traditionally the land for the people of Nepal and the very beautiful life they currently have – mostly due to tourism and their ability to farm – could become the next iron ore, uranium, or copper mine for the Chinese; and the majestic rivers that flow to the Nepalese plains could be a convenient dumping ground for mining tailings or a hydroelectric plant to send power back over the Himalayan range to China. May the gods never allow such a thing ... but look what happened in Tibet.

Historically, the gods have allowed such things. In my homeland of Australia, within the last 250 years, our government has sanctioned the destruction of indigenous people through taking of their land, shooting, poisoning, rounding up and chaining them, and taking their children away. Is it no wonder several generations on from those times that the indigenous people still struggle with assimilation. As if it could be any different after the terrifying treatment they received from us 'white fellas' all in the name of 'King and Country' in the early days, and extending even to the very racist culture of the 1960s, 1970s, 1980s. Even now – in 2018 – I have heard such disrespect for our own indigenous people who have cared for this land for over 60,000 years.

Our current federal government has even shunned protests by school children on the very real issue of climate change. I'm just not feeling so patriotic when our youth are condemned for speaking out about these very real issues.

This trip for me was about seeing the sacredness of the Himalayas and the people that have lived here for at least 5,000 years. Buddhism has been their mantra and connection to the land and universe, and every time they go to renew the flags or burn their juniper leaves they are connecting themselves to a way of life that we in the West (and let's be real, certain big Eastern neighbours too) sadly lack. We don't connect to the planet as the traditional cultures do; perhaps that is why 60,000 visitors per year come to the Annapurnas, to escape the West. I have my hand up and it's still waving!

We spent one more night in Manang in the comfort of our very lovely timber hotel. I always checked for an escape route just in case a fire ever started; judging how far the kitchen was from my bedroom – at least fifty metres – it was an unlikely threat, but nevertheless I decided the rear terrace without the handrails was the best probable exit point - even if two storeys up.

ABOVE: *Boys playing in Manang*
MIDDLE: *Store holder in Upper Pisang*
RIGHT: *Sunrise en route to Tilicho Tal Lake*

Day 6 and we were off, heading slightly west-northwest on a high track to Tilicho Base Camp, where we were to stay the night in preparation for visiting the famous Tilicho Tal Lake – the highest lake in the world for its large size of four kilometres long by one kilometre wide.

Once we reached an elevation of just over 4,000 metres the trail crept along at that contour with wonderful views down the valley. We had come to where Annapurna I, the highest peak in the region at 8,091 metres, loomed into view. Below us was the

Khungsar Khola River that flowed into the Marsyangdi Nadi, and then down to the lowlands of Nepal.

It was on this section that we saw several groups of blue sheep and about a dozen 'pretend' yak; by this I mean they are just a few genes removed from the wild yak but still very handsome with a lovely thick coat, several hundred kilograms of meat, and the ability to produce vast quantities of yak milk – which equals yak cheese, among other things. We were several hours trek from any village but they were quite clearly owned by someone, with their decorative coloured neck bands and metal bells. What's more, they were quite happy for us to go within a metre or two of them, which suggests they are well cared for and handled with gentle respect.

PREVIOUS PAGE: *Suspension bridge, west of Manang, en route to Tilicho Tal, 4,920 metres above sea level*

ABOVE: *Khangsar Kholo river, heading up to Tilicho Tal*

MIDDLE: *A yak...even if a few genes removed from the full blooded ones that now can only be found on the Tibetan Plateau*

RIGHT: *Nepalese lads from Pokhara up for some spiritual sun baking and fun!*

Within two hours walk of the Tilicho Base Camp there were many scree falls that ran for hundreds of metres down to the river. It was not a place to linger and so we kept up a steady pace for the next several hours. It would be sheer bad luck to be caught in such a scree fall, and lingering just added to the likelihood. So, on we pressed to the hotel known as Tilicho Base Camp, arriving late afternoon. There was snow and ice everywhere in the hotel courtyard, a two-storey timber structure just waiting for a fire to start somewhere, I felt. I was given an upstairs room and immediately developed an escape plan, being Christopher cautious!

Having a shower meant removing one's warm clothes – there was no heater and the likelihood of the pipes thawing from the previous night was pretty slim. We were after all at 4,150 metres, and it was December in the Himalayas. I just loved saying that: Himalayas! It just stirs my adventurous, wilderness seeking soul!

As early evening drew on to night the temperature dropped to minus five degrees, which meant the night was probably going to get to minus ten. All the guides and hotel crew were in the kitchen around the warm gas fires and general warmth of such a small space. There were ten or more of them while we paying guests, perhaps a dozen of us, sat around a cold steel fire drum where there was no fire and no heat. One of the guests asked for a fire to be lit at 5pm: as 5.30pm came and went, a Danish man and I decided to take the fire-building duties into our own hands … big mistake!

We knew where the firewood stack was and proceeded to load our arms with US$20 worth of firewood – or so we were told by the hotel manager who had placed a 'security guard' by the door to ensure we recalcitrant guests behaved ourselves. The issue is that everything has to come in by horseback; there was no firewood at these high altitudes, and apparently we had violated the Geneva Convention on 'good guest behaviour'. Akash came over and quietly lectured me on being a good guest, and said that I needed to see him if there was a problem. I tried to say that I didn't want to disturb his 'guide-buddy time' but he wasn't going to swallow that one. We were clearly in the wrong, they were clearly in the right; this was their hotel in their country and we should behave ourselves even if that meant sitting in the hotel lounge with eighty percent single pane glass all around in below freezing temperatures while they had their usual guide-time happy hour! Put up and shut up was the message, even if we were the reason they were earning the tourist dollars! Shiver we must!

Dinner came eventually and I decided to head to my room to make some notes and prepare for tomorrow; I had never trekked to 4,920 metres. We were to leave at first light on a trail that was to take three hours with a further elevation of 770 metres, and we were to return the same day. The weather was promising, with a low fog to start with. There was much snow and ice on the track, and the elevation was also a challenge. For the first time I felt the hard effort of breathing as my body did its best to take in enough oxygen to feed my hard-working muscles. There is nothing to do but walk steadily, stopping only when required, but always moving forward. To sit down at this point would be a big mistake as the body is likely to say: "That's enough, back to the hotel for beer and crackers and cheese and a good book sitting around the fire". Except the fire wouldn't exist where we were, nor would the crackers, cheese and beer.

At times I did feel I was on a five-star trekking tour as the food had been excellent, and the small cabins complete with bed, mattress, and quilt were always clean and free of any bedbugs, but maybe that was more to do with sub-zero temperatures than good management. The bathrooms were often problematic with water spraying or dribbling out in various directions, but even at these altitudes hot water was usually available. There was almost always a light in the centre of the ceiling and it usually worked, and the rooms were certainly very clean. But of course, at these altitudes the water pipes need to be insulated to keep them from freezing and that seems to be a rare event in the Himalayas – unfrozen pipes. However, I would give the trip a five-star trekkers rating, and the staff were mostly very friendly, except if one tried to pinch their firewood. What was I thinking?

Tilicho Tal Lake was every bit as spectacular as I had imagined. It had a crusty ice surface that may have held the weight of an average size dog, but its expanse was what most impressed me – all four kilometres of it – which was fed by a very large glacier some two kilometres wide. It had formed over thousands of years with water from Tilicho Peak, some 7,134 metres above the lake and not visible on this particular foggy day.

There was a group of seven young Pokhara men out for a few days to visit this natural masterpiece that was in their backyard, so to speak. They asked me to take lots of photos of them as a group, with their shirts off and their chests puffed out. Some of them really got into the Vladimir Putin look of machismo. But they were a fun group of young men enjoying their days off. One of them played a flute which resonated across the soft snow.

It was not a place to linger because of the cold, and we planned to get back down to Shri Kharka, a solid six hours walk back the way we had come the previous day. We passed over the massive scree slopes without any major slippages, and walked back over the suspension bridge to the small village of two hotels. Being Day 7, I decided it was time for a shower, with the owner guaranteeing hot water. What I didn't bank on was the little shower room made of stone and concrete with condensation that formed in a crusty ice lining. Once the door was closed it was pitch black because there was no electric light anywhere!

I bolted back to my room, which was up two flights of timber stairs. I got my torch and ran back down to the icy dungeon where I enjoyed a hot shower. Once the hot water was turned off, it was so cold it definitely wasn't five-star. I dried myself as quickly as possible and threw on my clothes for the dash back up to my room where I bolted the door, put on my usual five-layer clothing system complete with beanie and neck warmers, and dived under the quilts to thaw out. It took nearly an hour to feel like I was a warm-blooded human being again, albeit curled up in a foetal position. Showers from now on were off the agenda at this altitude; besides, it was winter in the Himalayas – a no sweat zone, at least compared to the tropics.

Day 8 and we were climbing to Thorong High Camp at 4,925 metres, which is where this story began at Day 9 with the freezing conditions that would see all ten of my fingers with a mild yet very painful case of frostbite. It would be several months before my fingertips thawed out. I was imagining myself with numb fingertips and flaking skin trying to write this story, not able to feel the keys and typing ludicrously spelt words.

> **IT'S NOT ABOUT HOW MUCH YOU DO BUT HOW MUCH LOVE YOU PUT INTO WHAT YOU DO THAT COUNTS.**

MOTHER TERESA

CHAPTER 05

YELLOW SYMBOLIZES EARTH

ARRIVAL IN KATHMANDU

"MY NAME IS CHELLIS AND I'M IN RECOVERY FROM WESTERN CIVILIZATION."

Chellis Glendinning

MY ARRIVAL IN KATHMANDU

On my arrival in Kathmandu on 3 December 2017, I walked through the terminal and was greeted by a young Nepalese gentleman wearing a grey suit, with an off-sider, presumably to carry my trekking pack. I was very polite but had no intention of being drawn into his sales web. It was no surprise he offered guided tours to the very place I was planning to go, Annapurna. His English and manners were excellent, but I still had a plan to get to my hotel in Thamel in the north-east of the city where I would contact the two guides I had been in touch with from Australia, that friends had connected me with. Even though these contacts were still on hi-season rates I thought I needed to touch base and bargain with them.

Kewal was the name of this young, well-dressed gentlemen; he ran a trekking company in Kathmandu, and there was virtually nowhere in Nepal he didn't operate. He walked with me at a very good pace as I had been sitting on a plane for over eight hours; we walked through the airport and down to the taxi rank where he opened the door for me with the greatest of courtesy. What was I to do? Go with the natural Nepalese flow? Of course!

I looked at this young man in his early thirties and decided that he was either a great con-artist or he really did have everything he told me about to offer. My defences weakened as I thought I may as well get a local quote; what's more, he was offering a ride to my hotel, as his office was just a kilometre away … coincidently!

Does one just trust or does one flow against the tide of life and the gifts that were being offered? I decided to trust! It was an hour's drive through heavy traffic that weaved through very busy streets that had some asphalt and many, many potholes. The roads were full of cars, taxis, scooters, buses, trucks carrying police and building materials, and somehow there was a gentle order to it all. The drivers just seemed to know what to do, and there was certainly a courteousness about the journey forward. Now, having

LEFT: *Swayambhunath Stupa, west of Kathmandu*

spent time with the Nepalese people, I understand their religion to some degree, and I can see how this traffic system worked. It could be described as a Buddhist process in life – gentle, with respect and with courtesy.

The buildings were three storeys at most, and of brick construction. I found the power lines which ran along the roadside on steel posts most extraordinary, especially where they came to a junction – kilometres of black wires laced together into all sorts of interesting shapes. Somehow it must have worked, a bit like the traffic!

We got to Kewal's office and his off-sider carried my backpack up the two flights of stairs, where I was offered tea, fresh water … a back massage… anything to loosen this wealthy Westerner up! I was joking about the back massage. There were several other offices with men working in them who were very friendly towards me; and why wouldn't they be? This was one big happy tourism family running on imported US dollars.

I put my prejudices aside to see what Kewal could offer me in terms of my plan to spend twenty-one days in the Annapurna. After nearly two hours of discussion he came up with a plan and a price tag of US$50/day, which included the bus to and from Pokhara, ACAP (Annapurna Conservation Area Project) fees, accommodation and food for the twenty-one days and, of course, a guide.

What it didn't include was a crafty labyrinth of extra teas, coffees, beer of course, cold drinks, hot water, Wi-Fi in some places but not all, extra food, and any porter's fees. How could any of that become a problem? Well, it wouldn't as long as you didn't complain or see the need to keep a close eye on the 'extras'. God forbid if you should question their Nepalese honesty!

I was keen to walk to my hotel and think this all over – it had, after all, been an over 9,000 km journey from Australia. Kewal very kindly offered to have one of his people walk me to my hotel, the Kathmandu Garden House in north-west Thamel, which was about half an hour from Kewal's office. In almost every direction I looked I saw something interesting including the fruit stacked on display – and I mean really healthy fruit; mandarins, apples, bananas, pomegranates, pineapples, green vegetables, carrots and a myriad of seeds of which I could only name a few; buckwheat, soy, and lentil.

I certainly didn't feel threatened as we walked – the people were friendly and no doubt very used to Westerners, although perhaps

a bit less so at this time of year. There was the usual developing nation rubbish very neatly swept to various points in the street. And then there was the suit shop that Kewal and his cohorts possibly shopped at. Kewal took great pride in his appearance and indeed rose above the squalor that still is a big part of Kathmandu; what's more, his price was less than the two quotes I had received via email. There was good money to be made in trekking holidays it seemed – especially to a smart operator like Kewal.

ABOVE: *The author on a roof-top café at Swayambhunath*
MIDDLE: *The Tibetan woman with her healing singing bowls*
RIGHT: *Mother and child at Swayambhunath*

We arrived at the hotel and my young guide shot off. Was a tip necessary? I did not know but he seemed very happy just to go. The moment I walked through the gate I was in love with this hotel. It was on the perimeter of Thamel, and so reasonably quiet. There was a beautiful private garden with lawn and shrubs and, of course, a Hindu shrine with marigolds and white cloth adorning it. I checked in for three days that I had booked online from Australia. There were perhaps a dozen other guests, and from the rooftop I could see many more hotels and a horizon of buildings that stretched into the haze. The population of Kathmandu is estimated at just over 1.3 million – goodness knows how the government counts them.

The afternoon was progressing, and I had agreed to meet Kewal for dinner near his office. I walked through the main shopping area of Thamel, with millions of prayer flags flowing above the streets. They looked so beautiful in their blues, white, reds, greens, and yellows and no doubt the need to bless this vibrant business precinct was very necessary on a daily basis. I most definitely knew I was in Nepal.

These streets were like lolly shops to me; hiking gear of every description – mostly filled with copies, of course, but I thought

RIGHT: *Stall at Swayambhunath*

some items might be safe to experiment with like socks, a 30-litre day pack, water bottles, and some clothing items. Most of these items had North Face stamped on them, which must infuriate the British company who generally charges what they like for their excellent equipment. But in Kathmandu there were copies galore and, in many cases, I got what I paid for, including a pack that needed additional stitching to connect the metal frame – something a genuine North Face product simply wouldn't use; a jacket that looked good but needed waterproofing; a one litre water bottle that leaked; and a lot of clothing items that kept the sun out, only! Sucker plus some, I reflected!

I met up with Kewal feeling mellow from my long flight and, of course, the beer he was so kindly offering. I think he knew he had made a sale even before I rocked up, and I had pretty well decided to go with him as his price was competitive, even though it was a cheaper option to just go on my own. I felt a guide would be very useful and injecting a few extra dollars into the Nepalese economy would be a good thing too. And there certainly was an honesty about him; his staff seemed to greatly respect him. He showed me photos of his family and I am sure he faced all the usual challenges that a family can bring. Everything stacked up; he wasn't a con-man, but simply a business man with an entrepreneurial flair.

So after dinner, which I paid for, we went back to his office where I got out US$500 which I had strapped to my torso, and my visa card to pay the difference – a total of US$1,050, or US$50/day; perhaps extravagant by Nepalese standards, but quite affordable for we privileged types in the West. The deal was done.

I walked back through the busy shopping streets of Thamel, where the lights never seem to fade and the prayer flags remained above me in a crisscross formation of colour. I was most certainly in Kathmandu, and I had just paid for twenty-one days of trekking in the Himalayas where I would see mountains well over 7,000 metres, and rivers roaring with a width of several kilometres in places; that was a thrilling thought, to say the least!

Some of the hotels I passed were very upmarket, with white marble tiling and brass handrails, lifts in the lobby, and quite likely every modern convenience that any Western visitor could want – even taps that didn't drip, maybe. I was very happy where I was, though; the staff were friendly, the food was good, it was clean, and it had a lovely rooftop garden and an even lovelier private garden

courtyard; what's more, it was US$10 per night with an ensuite bathroom and the usual leaking taps. In most villages I am sure they still relied on buckets and pails, or a Gurkha-installed village tap if they were lucky!

I had three days in Kathmandu before my bus would take me to Pokhara, where I would meet my guide, Akash. Early in the morning of my first day in Kathmandu I caught a taxi up to the famous UNESCO World Heritage listed treasure to the north-east of the city, called Swayambhunath Stupa; affectionately nicknamed 'Monkey Stupa' because of all the 'fucking' monkeys that hang around and look ever so cute until they try to reef food out of your hand. I found them bossy, rude, and in need of a thorough culling with a twelve-gauge shotgun one late afternoon when the Gods were having an afternoon nap. A thousand monkeys would not have been noticed – except if the Gods weren't taking their afternoon nap at that particular time of the day – perhaps then it may be better to live and let live, I thought later; one doesn't wish to upset the Gods.

My driver dropped me around on the west side as he said it was the easiest way to approach the Stupa, although the pilgrim stone stairs – and there are about a thousand of them – approach the Stupa from the main east side. My route up was a gentle stroll through many tourist stalls and it was at the third stall that I found a Gurkha knife; a very elaborate weapon with bone, wood, and brass in the handle. I simply couldn't resist; I was thinking of it as a gift for my son with the idea of connecting him to his grandfather's love and admiration of the Gurkha military. I gave no thought at the time to Australian customs and the almost 300-millimetre steel blade that was certainly sharp; no doubt in the wrong hands it could inflict some horrendous damage.

Interestingly enough, when the time did arrive on 3 January 2018 to cough up my piece of weaponry, I had completely forgotten I was carrying it deep inside my pack. It struck me when I got home that maybe I should contact the police, but I was very sure they had far more important things to do, and really it was no bigger than a standard kitchen knife; besides, it was in very safe hands.

I had read about this Swayambhunath monument to Buddhists and Hindus alike, and I had seen photos of the extraordinary large white dome that represents the earth, and the orange colours patterned across in loops, but nothing had prepared me for the day of cultural education I was about to experience. The monument is on a hilltop site and dates back to AD460. The white dome itself is almost one hundred metres in diameter, with the constant run of prayer wheels packed with hundreds of prayers; they remain polished from all the hands that keep them spinning day in and day out.

There was a group of perhaps forty young Buddhist monks all doing the circumference walk in a clockwise direction. The boys were around ten years of age and all looked in very good health, with that sparkle of cheeky youth in their eyes. Their teachers were men in their forties – sadly there were no girls or women, but I am sure they were coming the next day or perhaps for the afternoon shift. As I mentioned earlier, there is much balancing of the sexes needed in Nepal but some women, including Western women, do wear the signature maroon robes and do become Buddhist monks. This has been especially true in the past twenty years.

At Kopan Monastery on the outskirts of Kathmandu they have been receiving nuns for almost forty years. There is currently a new accommodation there, with the ability to house up to a thousand nuns with their own meeting hall, dining room, and study facilities. It is the largest Tibetan nunnery in the world. I had the very good fortune to visit it on my very last day in Kathmandu, but more on that later. (30)

I walked around the Stupa in the clockwise direction, not always spinning the wheels but most certainly noticing the wonderful brass artwork both for sale and as part of the Stupa. I can describe them as dragons protecting the small temples that housed various deities. I walked around to the main eastern stairway, which disappeared several hundred metres to the base. To my left there was an area I would describe as a classroom, and the large group of junior monks I saw earlier sat around with their teachers waiting for the proceedings to begin. I caught the attention of one of the teachers and indicated I wanted to take a photo; he gave me a welcoming wave and so I did. It was such a beautiful sight to see these young boys in the safe hands of such knowing men. There were drums and flutes standing in various places, also waiting for the process to begin. I loved what I saw; men being leaders to these growing boys.

Everywhere, it seemed incense and yak butter lamps were burning; it was hard not to feel the intoxication and celebration of this

LEFT: *Marigold necklace salesperson*

spiritual life. The vibrant white-domed Stupa, some thirty metres in diameter, rises ten metres to a gilded metal spire where four faces of the Buddha stare out across the valley and the city of Kathmandu. The gilded metal spire has thirteen beehive-shaped tiers, which represent the thirteen stages humans must pass through to achieve nirvana, a place of perfect peace and happiness like heaven. (31) Prayer flags waved from the gilded apex to at least eight points stretched out well beyond the Stupa. A cloth skirt which hung just above the eyes and eyebrows flowed around the square base with green, red, and yellow colours.

There were more than a dozen temples of various sizes around the Stupa, a mixture of Hindu and Buddhist. There was much worship at these holy places, using the yak butter candles, marigolds, incense, and many prayers. The whole area seemed alive in the celebration of spiritual worship. I just soaked it up.

I walked away from the hustle and bustle of the Stupa in a westerly direction where there were many more stalls selling brassware; figurines of every description, door handles, radiant suns, Buddhas, prayer wheels, miniature horses, cats, snakes, pairs of hands, door knockers, dogs – the list went on and on. There were also stone carvers working on what I presumed to be prayer wheels, and for the tourists there were relief carvings of yaks, a smiling sun, and the word 'Namaste' – a respectful greeting in Hindu custom.

By mid-morning I was looking for a teahouse, which I found to the north of the main action. It was on three levels with a rooftop garden – the first two levels were gift shops selling yak woollen products and brassware. I stopped on the second level and found an array of brassware; beautiful brass suns, Buddhas of every description, and Tibetan singing bowls of many sizes – the largest being three hundred millimetres in diameter. Some were simple in design while others were highly decorative with intricate patterns and sold for hundreds of US dollars, even in Kathmandu. Some were handmade – the design is believed to have originated in China around the fifteenth century BC, making these designs at least three and half thousand years old. (32)

With their humble beginnings as grain scoops, over the centuries they have developed into finely tuned instruments of healing and, as I was to find out that morning, their vibrations can penetrate right through one's body. The lady who ran the shop explained the process to me, and it would take at least an hour for her to focus on the eight chakras using nine of her largest brass bowls. I lay down on a cloth on the shop floor and relaxed as she got each of the bowls up to a sonic intensity one by one. She then pressed them into each of my chakras and proceeded to find areas of my body that needed additional healing, like one of my knees and my lower back. I could feel the vibrations penetrating deeply and I felt the healing qualities throughout my body.

When she had finished I was in such a relaxed state I was no longer aware of my surroundings as the sound of the larger bowls were very loud, yet very soothing. I felt my senses heightened by the experience and when I eventually did come back to Planet Earth she suggested I needed a further eight sessions to really heal the effects of Western living. I wasn't going to argue with that; in fact, I was surprised it was not a further hundred and eight sessions. I thanked her very much and took my two purchases with me; a small brass Buddha, beautifully made, and one of the very lovely brass suns with a face depicting gentleness and sublimity; I'm guessing it was a Buddhist sun, and I truly loved it.

Other stalls had the most intricate and beautiful masks carved from timber, which are used in many of the festivals held throughout Nepal. Some are quite scary with their angry faces and gaping mouths and teeth and raised eyebrows. Others were more dragon-like with huge teeth, while some more sublime types represented elephants and gilded Buddha heads. The list and descriptions were endless, as is the imagination of the Nepalese people. This whole site represented a clear union of Buddhism and Hinduism. It is interesting to discover that Nepal is a blend of religions, with Buddhism making up only 9%, Hinduism 81.3%, Islam 4.4%, Kiratism 3.0% and Christianity 1.4%. (33)

Unfortunately, some peripheral buildings to the Swayambhunath had been damaged by the 2015 earthquake which rocked Nepal in many ways. An estimated nine thousand people were killed, and a further twenty-two thousand injured. The epicentre was east of the Gorkha district, some fifty kilometres north-west of Kathmandu, where most of the damage occurred and many towns were razed. The quake even triggered an avalanche on Mt Everest, one hundred and fifty kilometres from the epicentre, and killed twenty-one people in the process. (34)

Many buildings in Kathmandu of world heritage significance were very badly damaged; places such as Durbar Square, Patan, and Pashupatinath. They were on my visit list, but I discovered timber propping poles and wire fencing to keep visitors out. I am sure, however, that donations will get to the right organisations to repair these precious places of international significance. One can only imagine how terrifying such an earthquake would be to experience.

I walked down the long flight of stairs to the east of the Stupa. This was the main entrance but also the place for beggars which I found to be very disturbing – as does most anyone who witnesses such a thing in a developing country where begging is far more acceptable than in the West, where we have a welfare system. From a hundred metres away, I could see a woman gathering her children into position. They must have done this routine a hundred times – her sitting with the children on her lap, with everything about them spelling poor. I could have just handed over 100 rupees like most other tourists, but from previous experience in developing countries and an article I'd read (35) – in which they interviewed the director of an NGO (non-government organisation) called Dhan Saru, which worked with disadvantaged children in Nepal – I had a good idea of what the best thing was to do as a visitor. The simple answer is that the more they are given on the street the more likely they are to stay on the streets; even the gift of food contributes to this vicious cycle.

ABOVE: *Street market fish near Durbar Square, ready to go!*
MIDDLE: *Fruit and vegetable sellers, Durbar Square*
RIGHT: *Environmentally friendly bowls*

Dhan Saru recommends giving to or volunteering with a reputable aid agency such as the Nepal Youth Foundation (36) or a registered charity in Australia called The Pencil Tree Foundation – which focuses more on Tibetan children. Either way, these organisations are reputable and offer long-term solutions to helping future generations. In this way continuing support can be offered to these children rather than the quick fix of 100 rupees; stories abound of "pimps" controlling the lives of these beggars – children and adults alike.

I walked back to my hotel somewhat unnerved by what I had seen, and the lack of action I seemed to take; I decided I needed to do something positive for these children, and I would make a donation on my return to Australia. Seeing these things firsthand is a galvanising call to duty. These people need real and sustainable solutions – not a quick 100 rupee from a tourist, and there are positive solutions to be found with a little careful research, that will help them get off the streets permanently.

The following day I headed off early to walk to Durbar Square in central Kathmandu. Walking these streets included a cacophony of sounds, smells, and sights. I saw beef, chicken, and fish on the sidewalks, spread out on small tables, exposed to the daily grind of dust and dirt. The fish particularly concerned me as to its health specs. I decided to pass on a purchase and remain with a more durable meat like beef for all future consumption. On reflection, I am very pleased with the fact I didn't get sick the whole time I was in Nepal. The quality of the food generally is very good, and I always treated the water with chlorine tablets I had brought from home. Even the best mountain springs can end up with a dead monkey in them; it's just not worth the risk.

Road works were also of interest as they were dug up perhaps a hundred metres at a time and left open with next to no protection. It could have been sitting there for weeks, perhaps waiting for the right parts to arrive, but life just flowed around it and no one seemed to fall in. It was just part of life in Kathmandu.

The temples were on every street corner it seemed; some were very elaborate; some very simple, but they were all used on a daily basis to pay tribute to the gods whether Hindu or Buddhist. I went into the door of one temple to see two women and a man holding space for a ritual. There was a beautiful pressed metal altar standing nearly two metres high and adorned in marigolds, and in front of the man sitting there was a table of what looked like offerings, yak butter lights, and incense burners about four hundred millimetres high. Hanging from the ceiling were cast iron bells that visitors of the faith would ring when they came in; money would be exchanged, an offering was made, the bells were gonged, and out they would go. Life was celebrated, honoured, and appreciated ... now off to work.

Such a beautiful temple, and only about five metres square from the outside. The heavy brass doors were very impressive with a large eye on each leaf. There was such detail in the construction, with a vibrant community connection to something much bigger within the universe.

Durbar Square was within walking distance south-east from Thamel, and is a collection of twenty or more temples mostly Hindu in origin; regrettably many had been terribly affected by the infamous 2015 earthquake. There was so much to see and one of the most striking was a black and maroon building called Kumari Chowk. There was only a small portion of it open to the public due to earthquake damage, but the colour contrast and detail in the construction of its doors, windows, shutters, and brickwork was extraordinary to say the least.

ABOVE: *Garuda Stone Statue from 400AD, Durbar Square*
MIDDLE: *Kamari Bahal, abounds in female spiritual energy*
RIGHT: *Pomegranate salesperson near Durbar Square*

Despite the timber proppings found everywhere on the Kumari Bahal it was well worth a visit, with deep orange colours on the brickwork and rich black colours on the window openings. It abounds with female spiritual energy. It is the home of Kumari, a girl who is selected by the townspeople to become the living goddess until she reaches puberty, at which time she returns to be a normal human mortal. (37) The timber decorative work is striking to say the least; doorways with skulls carved all the way round at hundred-millimetre centres, and flowers done in a similar style. Above the door there is an arched carving rising a metre with all manner of female Hindu figures, some with seven pairs of arms; others to the side looked like mermaids and dragons with clawed feet. I think they were all meant to be here to protect this young lady, and the craftsmanship was exquisite.

Inside the courtyard was more of the deep orange painted brickwork, and around the jet-black woodwork of the archways were serpents of incredibly intricate designs. Under these were human faces looking down on the people walking below. More black skulls were below with female human forms in the shape of a shield at each of the transoms.

I was able to visit the five Hindu statues that were housed under a very low ceiling, with a friendly man keeping guard and politely telling me that being a foreigner I could only stand at the entrance, but I could see the small statues perhaps six hundred millimetres high that symbolised the components of the Hindu religion. A lovely warmth of community came to me while watching these people pay respect to their gods with marigolds and incense.

Outside and to the north-east was a timber temple set up on a stone plinth ten metres square. It was famous for the erotic carvings on each corner supporting rafter. I had read about these carvings but my goodness they were raunchy, with all manner of goings on and very little catering for the standard husband and wife; this was far more out there with three and more eager participants. It dated 1563AD and all manner of sexual fun was being had by multiple

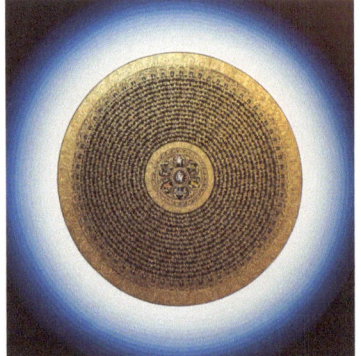

ABOVE: *Kala Bhairab, a popular Hindu figure from 400AD*
MIDDLE: *Art shop adjoining Durbar Square with a focus on the Universe*
RIGHT: *One of the many 400 year old erotic carvings found in Durbar Square*

partners. It begged the question; was this fantasy or fact 454 years ago? I wondered why two women wearing blue police uniforms and carrying automatic rifles were assigned to this site and this site alone; most bizarre, I thought, but perhaps the timber carvings were worth big money on illegal antiquity markets. It was certainly hot material and all part of a temple that was three levels of carved decoration; most creative and mindfully expansive! (38)

King Pratap Malla's Column dated back to the seventeenth century and had stood next door to this erotic temple; sadly, the top had been knocked off in the earthquake and pigeons had 'shat' all over it, just to rub salt into the wounds.

In many directions there were signs of intricate timber work, people selling marigolds and incense, large stone lions sitting two metres high. Out of the top windows of the Shiva-Parvati Temple there were two wooden carvings of human figures – the man dressed in white with a very charming moustache and gilded crown on his head, and the woman with a turquoise blue gown, red lipstick, large flower-like earrings, and a similar gilded crown. They were looking down on the people in Durbar Square with great promise and respect.

There were other Hindu carvings depicting human figures with pig heads and three pairs of arms; female forms with outstretched arms and others in meditative positions; other female forms playing the flute; timber carved decorations galore; and bells – lots of bells – about a hundred millimetres in diameter. The corner support posts in the form of a lion had a rather large phallic member, and the nearby women were dancing and men were sitting. It all needed a good washing down and oiling but hopefully money and skilled workers were on their way as these were priceless pieces from another time; hence the female police with automatic rifles – however I would be surprised if they were actually loaded or that this was a 24/7 stake out.

At the southern end of Durbar Square was a large stone Hindu carving three metres high with hands held in prayer and large wings attached to its back. It had the ceremonial blessings of marigolds, deep orange colours, and oils that had been sprayed over its midriff. It was a Garuda statue and had survived the quake. It is believed to be from the fifth century AD, and represented a leader from that time called Mana Deva. It was an extraordinarily impressive stone piece. (39)

In the Basantapur Square just to the east of Kumari Chowk was a major restoration project from the earthquake, called Hanuman Dhoka; it is Kathmandu's royal palace dating back to the fourth century AD, and was largely expanded in the seventeenth century. (40) There were also another four police dressed in dark blue uniforms and one with an automatic rifle – the illegal antiquity markets must be booming!

The Kala Bhairab was a very popular Hindu figure with the locals. They made offerings of marigolds, yak butter lights, incense and, of course, rang the big bell just behind his right side. This figure has the most fearsome pose with six arms, a garland of skulls, and he is shown trampling a corpse all covered in red ochre; the corpse being symbolic of human ignorance. I thought that was interesting! On each side of him were two white lions standing almost two metres high. It is believed that if one tells a lie in front of this fearsome

figure they would be instantly dead. It is believed to have come from the fifth century AD and is made of stone. (41)

To the west of this fearsome Hindu god I found an art gallery, but not an ordinary art gallery; the works were exquisite, representing the universe and all that shone from it. There was a radiance in these works I had not seen before; the power of life and no doubt death. They started at around US$200 and just went up depending on size; some were several metres across. I could have bought one there and then but for my restricted trekking budget, and the slight inconvenience of carrying it through the Himalayan Mountains. I would also have liked to offer US$1million to assist in the restoration of the very special Durbar Square.

I came across a small alleyway just off from the main Durbar Square and very close to where you could buy a dead chook, fully plucked and lightly singed, ready for the pot. I felt drawn to walk down this alley. It was so very low I had to stoop, but it was obviously used on a daily basis as there was no dust on the ground. It came out into a small open courtyard perhaps ten metres square, with buildings rising four or five storeys. The timber work, even though very old and very ornate, was in need of a good wash down and a thorough coat of a good quality wood preservative.

I wanted to climb to the top and get on with the job. However, I could hear families behind the timber screens and low doorways. There was a well in one corner with a brick perimeter about half a metre high, which didn't appear to have been used in recent times. I just took it all in. This was where whole families lived in Kathmandu, and most likely the apartments have been passed down from one generation to the next ... and it survived the fucking earthquake!

As I was about to leave an older lady came out into the courtyard and gave me a friendly smile. I felt somewhat guilty and awkward for intruding on her world – stickybeaking – but she certainly wasn't concerned at my presence. I was after all just trying to understand life in Kathmandu, and I certainly meant no harm to anyone. It was just one more interesting experience in this very old city, and I would guess the timber work went back to the seventeenth century. Nothing is more interesting to a trained carpenter.

I found a lunch spot at one of the rooftop garden restaurants to the south of the square, and really took my time to see what was before me; this remarkable historic Durbar Square, even if quite damaged by the earthquake, was teaming with life which spread as far as I could see – or, perhaps more accurately, as far as the smog and haze would allow me to see. But in every direction there was something beautiful, colourful, and decorative, whether it was a window frame painted bright blue, or terracotta roof tile decorations, or the people below dressed in bright blue, red, and green. And, of course, to the west was the famous Swayambhunath Stupa, mostly visible in the haze.

PREVIOUS PAGE: *Water well next to the Golden Temple, Patan*
ABOVE: *The Golden Temple (Kwa Bahal), a Buddhist monastery from 1100AD*
MIDDLE: *My helpful and cheerful guide at the Golden Temple*
RIGHT: *Guardian lion at the Golden Temple in Patan*

I took a taxi to the Patan Museum and was quoted 500 rupees for the ride, which is US$5; I thought it was probably on the tourist high side, but I let it go, I just wanted to get there. However, when we got there and I produced the 500 rupees, the driver said the bill was now 5,000 rupees or US$50. I said you must be joking, but it was obvious he was not! I got out of the car and slammed the door, making the point that I was not going to fall for that particular piece of tourist rip-off crap!

It was a forty-minute drive, but still I had some idea as to the correct price from my experience with the largely honest taxis I had used before. We did cross the murky Bagmati River which flows through the middle of Kathmandu; not a river that could be safely bathed in by any stretch of the imagination. It was the second dumping ground for rubbish; the first were the streets. Wheelie bins or any rubbish collection seemed another world away here.

However, since 2015 a Finnish and Dutch company has been involved in assisting Kathmandu with its rubbish problem. It is estimated that 1,000 tonnes of trash are produced daily in Kathmandu, and the majority of it is being transformed into a commercial fertiliser; the rest of it can be recycled as plastic, glass, and metal. Thank the Gods, a good news story by the Finnish and Dutch. **(42)**

There was lots of evidence of the earthquake across the square. The buildings were shored up waiting for foreign investment that I knew would be coming; the world and especially Europe are in love with Nepal, and help is offered in abundance. The problem seems to be that the Nepalese government hasn't had a good reputation for directing foreign monies in the right direction at the right time – but that is just what I have heard. The shutters came down on my computer when I tried to research it!

PREVIOUS PAGE: *Boudhanath Stupa at sunset*
ABOVE: *Marigold sellers at Boudhanath Stupa*
MIDDLE: *The sacred white elephant getting some last minute touch ups for winter*
RIGHT: *Feasting monkey at Pashupatinath*

However, the following websites did jump onto my page:

www.business-anti-corruption.com/country-profiles/nepal

www.quora.com/why-is-nepal-so-corrupt

www.bbc.com/news/world-asia-32817748

http://kathmandupost.ekantipur.com/news/2017-01-26/nepal-ranked-as-third-most-corrupt-country-in-sasia.html

www.abc.net.au/news/2016-04-21/still-no-rebuilding-program-one-year-since-nepal-earthquake/7344208

www.tinepal.org/events/nepal-still-among-the-most-corrupt-countries/

I walked into the museum. The entrance was an ornate gilded form with many Hindu symbols; a lion at the very top with hands holding what looked like serpents. In the corners there were dragon figures with elephant trunks and a Shiva form at the base with five pairs of arms. Flanking her was Ganesha, the Hindu god of new beginnings and remover of obstacles. This was all supported by more intricate timber work two stories high with terracotta brick between.

There was an open courtyard with a garden for vegetables and exotic plants, and a café opposite. Another deep well, lined in brick, was positioned near the garden. It too looked like it hadn't been used in a very long time. I walked upstairs to the main part of the museum where there were more naughty X-rated wood carvings dating back to the seventeenth century, but no armed police this time. In other cabinets there were various statues in bronze, terracotta, and brass. They looked mostly Hindu in origin, incredibly ornate and very old. One brass sculpture, standing six hundred millimetres high, was a very shapely naked feminine form surrendering herself in the natural embrace of her lover, but I am sure there were much more deeply spiritual events taking place there. I can only conclude her beautiful feminine form was shaped by the Gods!!

There were much older figures, some nearly five thousand years old in fact; their shapes were very simple, but nevertheless they were priceless in terms of Nepalese culture and history. There was a display on the creation and manufacture of a Buddha's head using clay; a relatively small one, about four hundred millimetres in height. The level of skill must only increase as they build larger models.

At one of the windows I watched the workers on one of the buildings that had been crumpled by the earthquake. It seems a miracle the museum survived as just next door was a total re-build, but they certainly had the project well in hand. Of course, they had five thousand years of building skill and culture behind them.

I walked on to find the Golden Temple just north of the square, and stopped to buy a very beautiful necklace from a woman nursing her grandchild. I had seen these pendants in many places, and they represented in the most intricate way the components of Buddhism; they were made from brass with turquoise and red stones, fifty millimetres in diameter. I was less than impressed when I got home to discover that they could be bought on the holiest of holy websites, eBay, who offered to deliver it to your doorstep for US$35 … and I thought I was buying some rare and exotic Eastern treasure that I could only find in the holiest of holy Buddhist places, Patan. They were known on eBay as Tibetan Buddhist Mandala om Healing Amulet Necklaces, but then I wouldn't trust eBay's interpretation; any description to make a sale, I would think. However, I did very much like my purchase which was less than a third of what they went for on eBay, and I didn't want to bargain with the grandmother. I just hoped junior received new clothes from the sale.

The Golden Temple is a very unique Buddhist monastery dating back to the twelfth century (43) and remains remarkably unscathed from the earthquake. It is one of the most extraordinary buildings I have ever seen, with a central courtyard of about ten square metres and a smaller temple perhaps – five square metres – within, on a sunken platform. At every corner there were large dragon figures seated at two metres high, their mounting stand polished by the thousands of hands that ran over them on a daily basis, mine included.

ABOVE: *Kathmandu from Swayanbhunath*
MIDDLE: *Oh, I just hope the Buddhist monks don't get a taste for this – in full view of Boudhanath Stupa*
RIGHT: *The mesmerising yak butter lights – the feeling for me was a gentle and loving euphoria*
FAR RIGHT: *Young buddhists monks having a texting break at Boudhanath*

The whole central temple was gilded and open on four sides to receive gifts of incense, yak candles, and marigold flowers. The roof rose to an intricate apex with four serpents and an eight-sectioned pinnacle which in all must have taken several generations to build. This was a monument to Buddhism, and I'm very sure the young woman who led me through the temple told me the Dalai Lama visited here and that a ceiling dome was placed in his honour. It was a dark maroon colour, covered in Sanskrit and more than three metres above my head as we were walking out. I didn't understand whether my guide meant the current Fourteenth Dalai Lama, or one of the previous thirteen. All would fit into a twelfth century monument working on a fifty year per generational cycle. What I was certain about was that in every direction I saw great beauty in terms of the building, but also the pride, dedication, and most of all love the Nepalese have for their religion. It is a very heartfelt feeling to come away from something as beautiful as the Golden Temple of Patan.

Behind the main entrance stood twelve metres of a three-level structure which housed the main temple. It was a fully gilded band, some three hundred millimetres wide from the apex to the temple

LEFT: *Yak butter lights with their mesmerising powers of inner peace at Boudhanath*

entrance below. On the lower level there were four much darker figures about a metre high, with ten arms and decorations above, which I couldn't make out, but the bells were everywhere along the fascia; perhaps twenty or more. I'm not sure how anyone got up there to ring them, but I'm guessing it would have to be the gods. Perhaps the large bell at the entrance to this made up for it, being six hundred millimetres in diameter and probably weighing 0.5 tonne at least.

The next level had six similar-sized female figures with ten arms and above them what looked like garlands of flowers. They were gilded and struck the coolest pose, leaning on their left legs. And again, another row of at least twenty gilded bells. There is just too much ornate decoration to describe here except to say it reflected the Nepalese's deep love for their religion, culture and life.

On the final level, there were latticed shutters right the way across the building with the bells stretched along the fascia. It was easy to see why this was called the Golden Temple. The entrance to the main temple was guarded by two crouching elephants and two very fierce looking lions with rather large teeth, all in brass. In fact, savage lions with huge teeth and a large bell and chain around their necks featured prominently in this temple. A gilded doorway on the west side was also almost too much to describe, but the chicken-like figures with very large mouths and rhino horns – all gilded – were certainly worth noting. These treasures were featured along with eight other relief works. The gilded doors below and the beautiful feminine form that sat firmly in the middle was highly polished by so many visiting hands.

Just outside the main entrance to the Golden Temple was another water well almost two metres in diameter, lined in brick with a very attractive fern growing down the surface. I could see water in the bottom about ten metres below, and there was a rope that appeared to be attached to a bucket. Maybe this is where the holy waters are pulled from, but I have to confess I was not about to send my water bottle down for a top-up.

On the walk back to my hotel in Thamel I passed a shopping centre that had a six-metre-high Christmas tree out front. It was beautifully decorated in all the right ways; lots of gold, red, silver, blue, and green balls. For some reason I had the irresistible urge to chop it down and distribute the firewood throughout the poor people of Kathmandu. I really didn't feel this thing belonged here; I had

RIGHT: *The Buddhist chanting is soon to begin at Boudhanath Stupa*

chosen to fly over nine thousand kilometres to get away from the commercialisation of a Western Christmas. Luckily, they didn't sell axes or chainsaws in the shopping centre or those lovely police ladies with the semi-automatic weapons could have been after me. But I was very sure this shopping centre sold many things we don't need, in the name of Christmas.

The following day I was to catch my luxury bus north-west to Pokhara, and so begin my "Twenty-one days in the Himalayas". This was to be a scary drive with many signs of previous bus accidents littered along the roadside – not to mention the one that had careened over one hundred metres down to the river where a large number of passengers had been killed only several months before.

One of my excursions in Pokhara was to the World Peace Pagoda. I hired a brightly coloured boat complete with oarsman, a signature of Pokhara and Phewa Tal Lake. It was a solid hour's paddle across the lake during which I nearly bound and gagged my oarsman as he kept whining about how poor he was, how rich I was, and how he couldn't feed his family. I very nearly jumped overboard to swim the last five hundred metres; anything would be better than listening to his whining, but then I was no expert on fresh water aquatic life and the size of their teeth in Nepal, so I felt it best to knuckle it out to the end!

Nonetheless, the boat trip was very beautiful, with the Himalayas to the north-east and the reflections of the mountains and town in the water. Even though it is a large tourist destination I was seeing it at the quiet time – it was so very romantic and a beautiful place to be.

I met the trail that would take me to the summit, a solid hour-and-a-half walk with many steps through a rather lovely, temperate jungle. When I first saw the Peace Pagoda I was struck by the very beautiful and perfectly proportioned white design. It was built by Japanese Buddhists who had started the project soon after World War II. This particular pagoda is the seventy-first to be constructed around the world. It has a 110-metre diameter at the base, with a second tier of fifty metres, and a cylindrical top with a diameter of at least twenty metres. In all it stands over thirty metres high and at each point of the compass – north, south, east and west – there is a gold image of Buddha; spectacular in every sense. (44) From four or five points on the apex flew Tibetan prayer flags just topping off the perfect beauty of this structure and the hopefulness it projects to the world.

LEFT: *Boudhanath Stupa*

Ironically, when building work started in 1973 the Nepalese government had not agreed to it, and the work was quickly demolished. It took almost twenty years for the Japanese Buddhist monks to negotiate with the Nepalese government to continue. The government eventually agreed and a memorial was erected nearby with the Nepalese Prime Minister of the time, Girija Prasad Koirala, blessing the project – thank the Lord! … I mean Buddha! (45)

Being at 1,100 metres above sea level the views were peaceful, uplifting, and exciting; before me to the north-east were the Himalayas and in particular the Annapurnas. In the foreground was the large lake Phewa Tal, some five kilometres long by one kilometre wide, with Pokhara township spread along the shores. The colourful boats operated all over the lake, and at night were tied up in the pattern of a leaf; hence the popular tourist photo, and perhaps a trademark of Pokhara itself.

I had planned to visit one of the many Tibetan children's orphanages that existed around the perimeter of Pokhara. A friend of mine who runs the Pencil Tree Charity in Australia gave me the contact, but the day I was trying to organise a visit was in fact a voting day and every business, including taxis, were closed. Perhaps the politicians fear that no one would bother to vote unless a whole day is dedicated to their fine services, or something like that perhaps. But alas I never did make it to the orphanage where, while still in Australia, I had offered my carpentry services to repair school furniture. A noble deed I do intend to offer again one day; mountains and trekking and a deep appreciation for the Nepalese culture got in the way this time … very sorry! But I have not forgotten.

It's just a simple fact that one must visit Nepal for several months to truly appreciate it; the trekking is superb, as is seeing and understanding the culture. I thought sixteen days would be enough in the Annapurna, but I was wrong – I needed twenty-one days, coupled with the cultural sites of Kathmandu, and my trip was spent. But return I will!

POST-TREK

When I returned to Kathmandu from Pokhara in the luxury coach liner provided by Kewal – I found a hotel just ten minutes' walk from the World Heritage listed Boudhanath Stupa to the north-east of the city. It is the largest stupa in the world and pulses with life, as thousands of Buddhist pilgrims come to circumnavigate and spin the sacred prayer wheels which surround the base, which is over

200 metres in diameter. It is stepped around the main dome, with three further steps rising at least two metres at a time. Each step is decorated with marigolds in gentle waves. At the brilliant white dome, which is decorated with an orange colour also in a wave pattern, the four faces of the Buddha look out over the people. There is a skirt of coloured cloth around the forehead, and then the thirteen steps of enlightenment progress to the apex, all in gilded metal. Four bands of prayer flags containing twenty or more individual strands of prayer flags are tied down to the corners of the base. It is as beautiful as any European cathedral I have ever seen. (46)

It was built in 600AD and forms part of the ancient trade route that connects Tibet to Nepal; the need for the people to top up along the way with prayers, food, and inner strength was essential for the crossing of the Himalayas. In the fourteenth century Boudhanath was destroyed by Mughal invaders who spread across the Indian sub-continent at that time. (47) From that period of history, the Boudhanath has grown into what it is today; a living, breathing spectacle of Buddhist philosophy that caters over and above to every sense of the human body, and no doubt the thousands of pigeons that call this place home; surprisingly, it's not covered in pigeon shit. There must be very special people that take care of that particular natural phenomena. (48)

In the morning I would walk around the perimeter where there were three large groups of Buddhist monks gathered – mostly men and boys, but certainly some women too. They were all dressed in their maroon robes, some with gold and many with prayer books. Some of the boys had shaved heads, and they all sat cross-legged on the pavement facing the Boudhanath. The boys behaved as boys behave anywhere in the world, cheekily laughing with their friends until the prayer chanting started, led by a senior priest – or Bhikkhu – who was sitting on a higher platform; the amplified sounds of the prayers could be heard for miles. This happened at three points around the perimeter. I loved to watch the playfulness of the boys, and many were happy for me to take their photo, along with some of the older men. (49)

The second layer of this beautiful art form was whitewashed and so very clean considering all the activity – both human and pigeon. Small groups of older people were making the long threads of marigold flowers in preparation for when the current ones withered, and in an area between where I stood and where the monks chanted was a place that women did their protestations on a slat of timber

RIGHT: *The Cremation Ghats next to the Bagmati River, Pashupatinath*

the length of their body. This is quite a physical activity and it repeated for an hour or more at a time; the student surrenders to Buddha using her body to touch the ground in five places. As a student performs these protestations, she surrenders herself to the Buddhas of past, present, and future and ten directions. (50) It is not hard to fall in love with these people and the way they conduct themselves through their religion. I think that's the third time I have mentioned this...

In the early evenings just before sunset the trays of yak butter candles are brought out on large trays about half the size of a dinner table. They were lit by anyone wanting to pay homage to the Gods, and as they got going they began to glow in every direction. On numerous occasions I stopped to watch the people, mesmerised by what I saw. As I looked into the dozens of glowing candles – each so intense to look into individually – and then passed my gaze down the rows of literally thousands of these lights, it was easy to imagine we were in the hands of the Gods. I managed to take numerous photos of people who, just like myself, were transfixed by this Buddhist ceremony that happens every night of the year and has done so for thousands of years. Now that is a deep culture!

ABOVE, MIDDLE & RIGHT: *Hindu yogi's of Pashupatinath*

When in Kathmandu a visit to Pashupatinath is essential; it is a bit like visiting the Crown Jewels in the Tower of London but just slightly more 'in your face', shall we say. It is predominantly a Hindu site on the not-so-clean Bagmati River. There are ten ceremonial brick Ghats that are built right next to the river with the sole purpose of burning the dead and sending the ashes down into the river, which is more like a large creek; it can be said that most body parts do make it to ash depending on the skill of the fire master and 'jobs for the day' so to speak!

There were some temples where an armed guard would meet me with a mostly gentle: "Bugger off Western tourist, this is holy Hindu ground". I thought the semi-automatic weapons were a little unnecessary yet again!

There were many temples hit by the 2015 earthquake with the standard boarding bracing them. It was beautiful to see so much ritual with very large groups of people being blessed with marigold necklaces, incense, and face markings. A truly lovely and peaceful human experience. The slaughter of the bullock was less peaceful though. I arrived just minutes after the event, and blood was flowing in every direction. The head had been removed, and two men were busy gutting this enormous beast. They had many large bowls to collect the entrails, but little attempt was made to clean up the blood; I suspected it was part of the blessing and ritual for this most treasured animal to spill his blood in honour.

What I did find interesting was the Hindu Sadhus [51] who were offering blessings to tourists. They were dressed in very elaborate gowns of white, gold, and fawn with a hairstyle to die for. Some were quite elderly men and so had dyed their hair orange; their beards were tied in a long bun and many had a grey swirl of dreadlocks up to two hundred millimetres high. It was a very impressive sight, but it was at times difficult not to think they were there more for the tourists and the likelihood of a rupee exchange for a photo opportunity. I even came across one sneaking a cigarette in a nearby "yogi cave". [52] He was not impressed that I photographed the fag hanging out of his mouth. But I'm sure cigarettes do offer spiritual insight when they are away from Western tourists.

Nearby there were eight smaller temples all in a row, about four metres square and just as high. They had the most beautiful carved stone decorations that I imagine dated back to the early years of this very sacred Hindu place, perhaps 500AD. It was the carvings above each of the arches that stood out to me. There was a lion figure at the apex with serpents on each side, whose heads could have been in the mouth of the lion. Below this, on each side sitting on a plinth, was a phoenix, and then just to the side of that was a female form with five serpents behind her head in a protective mode. Her hair was done up with a crown of flowers. She had her hands clasped at the waist and was holding some sort of amulet. Such detail carved in stone is extraordinary, especially as these figures are at least a thousand years old. And this was repeated on all eight of the small temples.

Oh! The monkeys were another feature of Pashupatinath. I quietly thought to myself that perhaps a hundred of these cheeky little fellows could replace the grandness of the bullock! But then one would have to be very hungry to eat a monkey; tougher than old boots for sure. Alas, my thoughts returned to a thorough culling using a silenced shotgun as they had at the Swayambhunath Stupa; nobody would notice if done quietly one night when the Gods are resting! One would just need a small army of volunteers to follow behind to mop up the monkey mess.

On my very last day in Kathmandu I walked to Kopan Monastery; a European couple I had breakfast with said I must go, and go I did! It was only a forty-five-minute walk from Boudhanath in a north-easterly direction through the busy streets of suburban Kathmandu; actually, it was more like an hour, and that's if you didn't get lost. The buildings stood out on a hilltop which looked out over Kathmandu; it was worth the walk just for the view alone. However, this was no ordinary Buddhist monastery; Western types were welcome to stay up to a month or more to learn more deeply what Buddhism is all about.

The main temple was very large, perhaps fifty metres long by nearly thirty metres wide, and had a most beautiful interior with a ceiling five metres high. I took my shoes off to join the last hour of a group of about thirty Westerners, and sat down on ample cushions to hear this Western woman, who I guessed was of European origin, speak. She spoke of our Western minds and how we had to purify them to find enlightenment, and the journey to get to this place. It seemed like a very logical journey and a more peaceful one than we are presently on, and hopefully more environmentally sensitive than where we are now.

I always did have a great respect for Buddhists, and this trip had only deepened that respect. I felt very clearly that the next time I came to Nepal I would have to spend a month here at Kopan, a month helping with furniture repairs at a Tibetan children's orphanage, and a month trekking, miles away from any tourists. Three months; sounds perfect; now that will be a very long story, indeed! 2019 may just be the year, starting in September!

On one of the eastern walls of Kopan Monastery I found this quote entitled *The true meaning of life*. "We are visitors on this planet. We are here for ninety years or one hundred at very most. During that period, we must try to do something useful with our lives. If you contribute to other people's happiness you will find the true goal, the true meaning of life". This quote, of course, belonged to His Holiness the 14th Dalai Lama of Tibet … before the letters were re-arranged in 1959 to read 'C.h.i.n.a'; very interesting how international diplomacy works in the twenty-first century, but then it is still somewhat akin to ancient times. We just use bigger and more powerful weapons these days. However, I found the quote by His Holiness to be truly beautiful and definitely a goal to aim for every day till I reach ninety, if I am so lucky!

To the north of the main temple there was a beautiful garden with two smaller temples and highly decorated fountains with Buddha heads, one of which was very angry with big teeth; this flowed down to eight arms holding decorations, all gilded. The crowning Buddha was the sublime one with rather large ears.

PREVIOUS PAGE: *The ashes end up in the Bagmati river below*
ABOVE: *Stone carvings on the Shiva Shrines*
MIDDLE: *Hindu sacrifice to the gods – just minutes before I got there*
RIGHT: *Marigold necklaces for sale – symbolising the vibrancy of the sun, passion and creativity*

One of the temples was about six metres square and rose to at least eight metres high; the crowning peak had the thirteen tiers of enlightenment, with a sun and moon on the very apex. A small gold Buddha measuring about three hundred millimetres stood in a cave surrounded by an array of elephants, lions, dragon horses, and fish serpents; crowning all this was a winged eagle with a red crown.

Other carvings that decorated the perimeter were part bird and part woman holding a large snake. Other recesses had the Buddhist lion dressed in white, with gold decorations and big white teeth. It was a spectacle of Buddhist beauty that must have taken eons to build and decorate. The smaller temple nearby was equally beautiful, decorated with blue, gold, and pink half-man half-bird figurines playing cymbals. There was another Buddhist lion with a large garland of treasures strung between his paws, and he looked like he was doing a scary dance with all those teeth.

The top section had four rows of gilded Buddhas with hundred-millimetre centres, and they diminished in size with each row; but certainly not in impressiveness. There was also a pink horse about to break into a trot with a decoration of flowers and a red flaming headpiece on its back. Its expression was that of eagerness and being there to serve. On each corner was a warrior figure in gold and black. He was holding what looked like a sword, and wore a helmet with a large row of teeth across the forehead. The expression he wore said "don't even think about damaging this temple". It never crossed my mind! Besides, there were no monkeys in earshot!

ABOVE: *Elderly women at Boudhanath*
MIDDLE: *Kopan Monastery, north of Kathmandu was started by Tibetan monks fleeing persecution in Tibet by the Chinese in 1959*
RIGHT: *Kopan Monastery Stupa*

I headed back to Boudhanath in the late afternoon and found myself a rooftop restaurant for a final celebration dinner; the following day I was to fly home to Australia. On two occasions during my stay in Boudhanath I was 'befriended' by women. I think the script went something like this: "Single man, Westerner, looks clean and tidy and has infinitely more money than we do, opportunity to exploit".

At first, I thought it was a genuine interest in showing me the sites of Boudhanath and some of the intricacies of the rituals here but, alas, in both cases the pressure was on to go back to my hotel. Now, the Lotus Guest House is not the place to go to impress a girl and I soon became disinterested in buying every commodity they obviously could not afford, so I tried to sneak off into the crowd but she found me. Plan B was to run – and it worked!

It was a delicate balance to not offend these women, but then I most certainly did not approach them for gifts and God knows what else. They were both very lovely, very charming, and in their thirties but I felt there were probably many other Westerners willing to open their wallets to every Eastern surprise available. My intuition however was to keep well clear, and I did!

ABOVE, MIDDLE AND RIGHT: *Some of the infinite details on the Stupa at Kopan Monastery*

NEXT PAGE: *Yak butter lights that burn every evening and seem to go on forever, a celebration of life in my eyes*

In conclusion, Nepal and the Himalayas are some of the most beautiful places I have been to on our planet. I will be going again, to volunteer at the orphanage, to do some Buddhist courses at Kopan Monastery, and to trek – perhaps to Everest Base Camp this time.

I hope you enjoyed this story and that it has inspired you to travel there and "be what you dare"! Now there is a Latin translation tattooed on my left shoulder – generations before me gave these words as our family motto: 'Esto Quod Audes'. I simply will keep trying to live up to this so my grandchildren can find their rightful place in the world. Please be sure you try to do what your forebears set out for you to do; for me there is no greater quest.

POSTSCRIPT

"THERE IS NO PASSION TO BE FOUND PLAYING SMALL - IN SETTLING FOR A LIFE THAT IS LESS THAN THE ONE YOU ARE CAPABLE OF LIVING."

Nelson Mandela

When I arrived back in Brisbane there was a heatwave with temperatures of thirty-five degrees and higher. It took less than two weeks for me to crash in a heap, partly from the heat but also because I had been on a Himalayan high (without any drugs) for most of my thirty days in Nepal. If it wasn't the mountains, it was the rich culture that I could see in almost every direction I travelled. On top of that, there had been some changes on the home front with the need for my almost ninety-year-old mother to go into nursing care. It was a period of great transition and much gentle nurturing for my own soul.

I became disoriented and confused within a week – my mind was most certainly distorting and out of balance. I checked myself into New Farm Clinic for nine days – the first time I had been in hospital in six years. Would I have not gone to the Himalayas to avoid this fairly minor difficulty? Not on your life!

MAP OF THE ANNAPURNA CIRCUIT, HIMALAYAS

LIST OF REFERENCES

(1) https://en.wikipedia.org/wiki/Muktinath
(2) https://en.wikipedia.org/wiki/Gambling_in_China
(3) https://en.wikipedia.org/wiki/Demographics_of_China
(4) https://en.wikipedia.org/wiki/Self-immolation
(5) https://en.wikipedia.org/wiki/History_of_Tibet
(6) https://en.wikipedia.org/wiki/Apis_dorsata_laboriosa
(7) Lonely Planet, Nepal, 10th edition, p.342
(8) Lonely Planet, Nepal, 10th Edition, p.342
(9) https://en.wikipedia.org/wiki/Shiva
(10) chrisbonington/goodreads.com
(11) Documentary: The Hard Way Up, The Annapurna South Face (1970) by John Edwards
(12) https://en.wikipedia.org/wiki/List_of_Mount_Everest_expeditions
(13) https://en.wikipedia.org/wiki/Timeline_of_Mount_Everest_expeditions
(14) www.ecohimal.org
(15) https://en.wikipedia.org/wiki/Ghandruk
(16) https://nepal.helvetas.org/en
(17) https://en.wikipedia.org/wiki/Gurkha
(18) https://en.wikipedia.org/wiki/Gurkha
(19) https://en.wikipedia.org/wiki/Snow_leopard
(20) https://en.wikipedia.org/wiki/Wild_yak
(21) http://content.time.com/time/world/article/0,8599,1592687,00.html
(22) http://content.time.com/time/world/article/0,8599,1592687,00.html
(23) https://freetibet.org/about/environment
(24) http://content.time.com/time/world/article/0,8599,1592687,00.html
(25) https://en.wikipedia.org/wiki/Buddhism
(26) www.deliriumsrealm.com/pretas
(27) Wikipedia.org/om_mani_padme_hum
(28) Wikipedia.org/prayer wheels
(29) Wikipedia.org/prayer flags
(30) www.kopannunnery.org
(31) Lonely Planet, Nepal 2017, p.118
(32) https://en.wikipedia.org/wiki/Standing_bell
(33) https://en.wikipedia.org/wiki/Religion_in_Nepal
(34) Wikipedia/Nepalearthquake2015
(35) Lonely Planet, Nepal p.95
(36) www.nepalyouthfoundation.org
(37) Lonely Planet, Nepal, p.67
(38) Lonely Planet, Nepal, p.72
(39) http://ecs.com.np/heritage-tale/garuda
(40) Lonely Planet, Nepal, p.74
(41) Lonely Planet, Nepal, p.72
(42) Nepali Times 27 Feb to 5 March, 2015
(43) Lonely Planet, Nepal, p.143
(44) wikipedia.org/wiki/Shanti_Stupa_Pokhara
(45) wikipedia.org/wiki/Shanti_Stupa,_Pokhara
(46) Lonely Planet, Nepal, p.128
(47) Lonely Planet, Nepal, p.128/129
(48) https://en.wikipedia.org/wiki/Boudhanath
(49) www.google.com.au/search?q=buddhist+priest
(50) www.buddhist-temples.com/buddhism-facts/buddhism-ritual.html
(51) https://en.wikipedia.org/wiki/Sadhu
(52) Lonely Planet, Nepal, p.125

ADDENDUM

> "HAPPINESS IS NOT SOMETHING READY MADE. IT COMES FROM YOUR OWN ACTIONS."
>
> Dalai Lama

This story cannot go unfinished without further reflection on my guide, Akash. It is unrealistic I feel, for two males over that period of time together to not find some level of conflict. I think it's called "machismo" and many wars over the centuries have been fought over this simple premise.

Akash was simply doing his job and he was very good at it; what's more, his English was excellent. And while I could have remained the lovely, polite little guest in a foreign land there were issues I could not avoid, especially in terms of all the little 'extras' that I was charged and only told about to a small degree, but not in enough detail.

In my very firm opinion these extra charges were designed to extract as much as possible from the 'wealthy' Westerner; however, if all trekkers just go along with this attitude, the Annapurna and other trekking highlights of Nepal would be soon at Hilton Hotel prices and even then you may have to pay extra for Wi-Fi, hot and, cold water, room heater, extra tea, extra food, and possibly toilet paper. Of one thing I was sure – the Himalayan air was not charged for – but I bet they have talked about it!

The estimate of tourists heading to the Annapurna alone is close to 60,000 visitors per year, mostly in April and October. One does not need to be an economist to know these people are doing very well out of this tourist trade, and indeed why not? What's more, the Annapurna and other high traffic areas see the best levels of respect for Nepalese women out of all Nepal. And I certainly met many such empowered women on my travels there – money being a form of power, especially in the right hands.

With that said, would I hire Akash again –or any other guide for that matter? Yes. Firstly it is good for the Nepalese economy, and all the people I came into contact with along the way. What I would do differently is pre-arrange a 'step off point' – by this I mean that after say fifteen days, the guide is to return home and I can trek ... ALONE in the mountains, where I can speak to the Gods!

I think Akash felt he had failed, but he certainly had not. I made a point of emailing his boss when I got back to Australia to say this was not the case, and that Akash was a very good guide. I would recommend Akash, but make certain to let him see you are writing down all the little extras. And for reference, when I left Kathmandu they were working on a 'Himalayan air rate' of US$12/day ... and it would be worth every dollar! Ha!

On a more serious note, a good friend of mine runs an Australian-based charity called "The Pencil Tree". Stevie Bellamy is his name and I have interviewed him on my little radio program *Men's and Women's Stories* which can be found on SoundCloud. Stevie has travelled to Nepal for over twenty years and established this charity just five years ago, with the sole purpose of suppling educational material to the exiled children of Tibet. You may recall in this story some of my feelings on this mass exodus directly caused by the Chinese government back in the 1950s. Stevie's charity is working towards assisting these often-orphaned children who now live in Northern India along with the Dalai Lama. One thing is for certain; the 14th Dalai Lama has no option to return to his home and birth country of Tibet, with China lapping within their borders.

Stevie's charity can be found at **www.thepenciltree.com.au** – I thoroughly vouch for Stevie's charity and the thousands of lives he has touched.

One final note; my fingertips did eventually regain their nerve endings and feelings – a small example of how things can go wrong, especially when I thought I had all possibilities covered. It's easy to overlook something minor – like outer gloves – especially if you are from Australia. Ha!

ABOUT THE AUTHOR

"THE GOAL IS NOT TO BE BETTER THAN THE OTHER MAN, BUT YOUR PREVIOUS SELF."

Dalai Lama

Photo by Imogen Easton 2018

I was born in Stanthorpe, south-east Queensland on the 9 October 1961 to British migrants, John and Diana Easton. I had two older sisters, Helen Coromel and Heather Jan Easton. For those of you who don't know Stanthorpe, it is very beautiful country rich in vineyards, orchards, a natural stone granite landscape, and many cultural events such as musical concerts and the bi-annual Apple and Grape Harvest festival.

We were there for three years, but as a young teenager we would return regularly to Stanthorpe to stay with the Stratton family just outside of town on a forty-acre farming block. Matt and Molly grew all of their own food and on occasion my father and I would help Matt slaughter and process one of his cattle. I am not sure of the brown-coloured breed, but the experience was invaluable to me as a young teenager partly because I was working hand-in-hand with my father and Matt all weekend, but also because I learned the process of preparing the meat and how to cure a skin. I would later go on to show my own son these skills in hunting feral animals such as rabbit, fox, deer, goat, and pig.

At the tender age of thirteen a grave tragedy struck our family; I witnessed my sister Heather fall to her death from "Lost World" on Lamington National Park's western plateau. It is aptly called "Lost World" because fifty metre cliffs surround this small land mass with two very narrow razorbacks being the only access – one to the east and the other to the west.

I could quite easily write another 20,000 words on this tragedy, the effects on my parents, my sister Helen, and of course on me. My father spent many weekends up on the plateau in this very beautiful and wild part of the world, often on his own but also with me. He installed a brass plague that is still there to this day. It reads:

ON THE 10 DECEMBER 1974

HEATHER JAN EASTON AGED 19 FELL TO HER DEATH FROM THIS CLIFF WHILE ON A FOUR DAY TREK WITH HER BROTHER TIM, KARL STAISCH AND FOUR FRIENDS WHO ALL SHARED HER LOVE OF THE GREAT OUTDOORS.

May her spirit watch over the bushwalkers who pass this way.

With the difficulty of understanding such a family tragedy I have searched deeply for answers. In my late thirties I sought professional help to understand the depth of my depression – and, of course, it was no surprise that it was directly related to the loss of Heather, but also to witnessing the deep grief both my parents suffered for the better part of twenty years.

The positive message for me in all of this had to do with a Wedge Tailed eagle who flew in so close to me as we sat on the cliff face waiting for help. I could feel this bird's wind spray from its wings. I had been falling in and out of shock that afternoon but I do remember this happening with the help of a dear family friend who was with me on this four-day trek – Nameer Davis. This magnificent bird has returned to me many times, not close enough to feel the wind from its wings but close enough to feel its power and grace.

My editor asked me: "So why did you do this trip – alone?" I can easily say for the deep love and respect for my very English parents and their sense of spirit and adventure. For my grandfather, who spent most of his spare time researching our deeply rooted Anglo Saxon history. The family motto in Latin:

"Esto Quod Audes" (Be what you dare!) most certainly plays into why I did it.

Perhaps also, at a very deep level, is my mother's 'education for me'. She went to a Quaker school in England for over five years, called St Christopher's in Letchworth, and by education, I mean her love and respect of other cultures and acceptance of other peoples, and most certainly a curiosity from her own travels and reading. My mother respected other cultures for what they were, unlike my father who supported British colonialism – a subject they would argue over on more than one occasion. It would often end with my mother yelling quite loudly ..."well why didn't you stay in the bloody army..." For an Englishwoman who rarely got angry this was prime material.

This of course contrasts with my very British Army father who spent five years at the tail end of World War II training to be an officer, and who served in Palestine and Southern Europe. My father was juxtaposed to my mother's education as he won a scholarship to Plymouth College and most certainly learnt to be 'British' at this school, with Sir Francis Drake 'walking the halls' and making his presence felt – especially on Plymouth Hoe where there is a very large monument to Sir Francis Drake. However, I learnt from my father the importance of discipline, and being organised and efficient when it comes to the nuts and bolts of such an adventure as this.

And why travel alone? I find I am more easily immersed with other travellers and the locals and, of course, there is the ability to move more quickly – not that reaching a destination is necessarily my goal; enjoying the journey is by far the most wondrous gift when travelling.

A good travelling companion is, of course, a blessing indeed and Rod Smith from BBW is one such friend – we did a twelve day trek in south-west Tasmania in January 2016, 16 days on the Larapinta in the West MacDonnell ranges, Central Australia, and in January 2019 we are doing the Arthurs in south-west Tasmania, another 16 day trek through some magnificent wilderness country.

My professional life started for me at age twenty-two when I won a carpentry apprenticeship with Griffin and Knowlman P/L based in the leafy green suburbs of Western Brisbane. They were a highly respected building company with some thirty years' experience when I joined them for a five-year term. The staff and contracting tradespeople were some of the best in terms of their workmanship, honesty, and professionalism ... and we had so much fun building these up-market homes – a camaraderie of good men.

By 2009 my world came crashing down with a mental illness that in 2012 was diagnosed as bi-polar disorder. With the help of a very good doctor and facilities of New Farm Clinic I have got my life back on-track, but it's been a long, almost ten-year journey that one can never really get over – one simply learns to manage the illness. There are perhaps 20,000 more words I could write on my personal struggle with this inherited illness. My concluding comments on this very challenging subject are that if you know someone with this illness to not write them off but rather try to understand what that person is going through – with the correct professional help it can be understood and managed. There is hope!

In 2000, while renovating two homes and with three small children in hand, I was based in Manly, Brisbane, and I graduated with a Communication Degree from Griffith University. I had been persuaded from the age of seventeen to write and I always knew I would complete majors in Journalism. I just didn't think I would wait until I was thirty-six – but I flourished at university, and I discovered that my gift was more in radio than writing. Hence from January 2014, for almost five years, I ran and hosted *Men's and Women's Stories* from Radio 4EB in Kangaroo Pt.

I managed to record over 150 one-hour stories, all of which currently sit in a SoundCloud for public access. For four years of this time I was the carer for my now ninety-year-old mother – a mutually beneficial arrangement in a time that I was building my strength and my mother's age was catching up with her wonderful spirit.

I hope you find this very real story of great interest and inspiration to you.

www.ingramcontent.com/pod-product-compliance
Lightning Source LLC
Chambersburg PA
CBHW042346300426
44110CB00032B/45